The *Art* of SUCCESSFUL MEETINGS

William Dixon Southworth, Ph.D.
Internationally Recognized Parliamentarian

Edited by
Martha J. Haun, Ph.D.
University of Houston

The McGraw-Hill Companies, Inc.
Primis Custom Publishing

New York St. Louis San Francisco Auckland Bogotá
Caracas Lisbon London Madrid Mexico Milan Montreal
New Delhi Paris San Juan Singapore Sydney Tokyo Toronto

McGraw-Hill Higher Education
A Division of The McGraw-Hill Companies

The Art of Successful Meetings

Copyright © 1997 by The McGraw-Hill Companies, Inc. All rights reserved. Printed in the United States of America. Except as permitted under the United States Copyright Act of 1976, no part of this publication may be reproduced or distributed in any form or by any means, or stored in a data base retrieval system, without prior written permission of the publisher.

McGraw-Hill's Primis Custom Series consists of products that are produced from camera-ready copy. Peer review, class testing, and accuracy are primarily the responsibility of the author(s).

3 4 5 6 7 8 9 0 HAM HAM 0 9 8 7 6 5 4 3 2 1

ISBN 0-07-059809-6

Editor: Judith A, Wetherington
Cover Design: Maggie Lytle
Printer/Binder: HAMCO/NETPUB Corporation

To my wife Violet who imagined it .....

To Allan Steinman who nurtured it ....

To Martha Haun who quickened it ....

FOREWORD

Every meeting that handles business has procedures - but what kind of procedures? Most every one knows how to start and end a meeting, but what happens between the first and the last rap of the gavel. Let's consider some bad examples.

The president of the garden club has been president for twenty years, so long, in fact, no one dares to suggest a replacement. During those twenty years he has worked hard for the club, carrying responsibility because, as he says, "No one else will do any work." That's not true. He has committee chairmen, willing to work, but he tells them what to do. He is benevolent, pleasant - so long as no one crosses him or asks questions. His favorite phrase is, "Trust me." He answers questions about changing procedures by saying, "We tried that once years ago. It didn't work. It won't work now. Don't worry about these things. Leave them to me. Just trust me."

At meetings he has procedures - his procedures. He stares down members who want to speak, ridicules reasonable questions about the club's business, and controls the meetings by heavy sarcasm that causes people to remain quiet rather than be embarrassed by this man.

The problem is well known - you all know a bossy old man who is the boss. Give him his way and he is gracious. Cross him and he is vindictive. The club has a problem. What to do?

Learn parliamentary procedure so that you can challenge the chair. Study parliamentary procedures, and the club's bylaws with other people of spunk. Determine - no matter how scared you may be - to secure your rights as members of the club. First, challenge a doubtful vote by shouting out, "Division." Have your parliamentary authority turned to the page that authorizes you as a member to have a standing vote. When the chair asks, "What the devil are you talking about?" read him chapter and verse.

Suppose the chair refuses to listen to you, and goes on to the next item on the agenda. Then, having planned your strategy before the meeting, have one of your group stand and say, "I challenge the decision of the chair." Again your presiding bull may become angry, but again, have your buddy read him chapter and verse from the parliamentary authority.

You and your group should sit together and confer constantly about your actions against the chair's tyranny. Don't be embarrassed, don't be put down, don't give up. Remember the chair is there to serve the entire group, not to serve himself. Be resolute because you are right. Rely on yourselves. Be prepared to holler back if you are hollered at. Remember, you have rights only so long as you are prepared to fight for them. If you are not, be sure others will use your rights as their own - and try to convince you they are helping you.

Don't be embarrassed, don't be put down, don't give up. You have rights only so long as you are prepared to fight for them. If you are not so determined, others will use your rights, and try to convince you they are helping you.

Parliamentary opinions are based on the latest edition of <u>Robert's Rules of Order - Newly Revised</u>, unless otherwise specified.

CONTENTS

Foreword	v
CHAPTER I Frequent Questions And Answers	1
Meetings	1
Parliamentarian	1
Voting	1
Nominations	3
Adjourn	4
Seconding	4
Quorum	4
Unanimous Vote	4
Unruly Members	5
Wording of Motions	5
Referring to Committee	5
Presiding	6
Point of Order	6
Point of Personal Privilege	6
Parliamentary Authorities	6
CHAPTER II Chairing with Confidence	7
Chairing with Confidence	7
Meetings Go Quickly When Chaired Efficiently	9
Effective Chairing Assures Meeting Success	11
Chair is Subject to Authority of Members Assembled	14
The Presider and the Parliamentarian - A Relationship	16
CHAPTER III Motions	19
Conflicting Motions and a Renewed Motion	19
Double Motions Are Clearly Best Off as Two Singles	22
Once Made, May a Motion be Withdrawn?	25
Dilatory and Improper Motions	28
No Motion, No Discussion	31

CONTENTS

CHAPTER IV   These Thirteen <u>Wrongs</u> Make For Thirteen <u>Rights</u> 34

These Thirteen <u>WRONGS</u> make for Thirteen <u>RIGHTS</u> 34

CHAPTER V   Meetings 38

The Ordeal of Hilda Hesser 38
Charlie's Meeting, Charlie's Rules 41
The Cookeville Birdwatchers' Society 43
Unfocused Meetings Destroy an Organization 48

CHAPTER VI   Subsidiary Motions 51

An Overview 51
Postpone Indefinitely 53
Amend 55
Substituting a Main Motion for Another 57
Substitute Motion Misused 59
The Secretary Erred - According to Hettie 61
An Error and a Myth 65

CHAPTER VII   Committees 66

Proper Use of Committees 66
Motion to "refer to a committee" gives time to investigate Committee 69
Handling Committee Reports 72
Discharge a Committee 74
Nominating Committee 75
The Committee of the Whole, The Quasi-Committee of the Whole,
and Consider Informally 79

CHAPTER VIII   More Subsidiary Motions 82

Scenario for "Postpone to a Certain Time" 82
Motion to Limit Debate is not a Debatable Motion 84
"Lay on the Table" Superior to "Previous Question" 86
Ira Harris' Distress 89

CONTENTS

Lay on the Table	91
Take From the Table	93

CHAPTER IX   Privileged Motions   **94**

Orders of the Day	94
Raise a Question of Privilege	96
Recess Starts Right After Its Own Motion Is Adopted	98
Adjourn - The Happy Motion	101
Adjourn Meeting to Another Specific Day and Time	104

CHAPTER X   Incidental Motions   **106**

Incidental Motions - An Overview	106
Appeal - All Kinds	108
Appeal	111
Requests and Inquiries	114
Suspend the Rules	117
Creating and Filling Blanks	119
Objection to the Consideration of a Question	122
Consider by Paragraph or Seriatim	124
Consider by Paragraph or Seriatim - Another View	126

CHAPTER XI   Reconsideration   **129**

"To Reconsider" strategy after close vote loss	129
Some Considerations of Reconsideration	131
Reconsider and Enter on the Minutes	133

CHAPTER XII   The Parliamentarian   **135**

Duties of the Parliamentarian	135
The Parliamentarian and the Olympic Committee	138
The Parliamentarian and the Tellers	141
The Parliamentarian and the IRS	144
The Parliamentarian as Expert Witness	146

CONTENTS

CHAPTER XIII MEMBERSHIP — 148

Membership — 148

CHAPTER XIV Voting — 151

On Votes and Voting — 151
Kinds of Votes — 152
Unanimous or General Consent — 156
The Flawed Election of Manager Mutz - Almost — 159
Voting for Church Council Membership — 160
Tellers Tabulating Tallies - Another Method — 162
Preferential Balloting - An Election — 164
Preferential Balloting - An Issue — 166
Mail Balloting — 168

CHAPTER XV Unusual Procedures — 171

Rescind — 171
Correcting Minutes — 174

CHAPTER 1 - Frequent Questions and Answers

Meetings

1. **What are the basic rules for a good meeting?**
   a. Develop a detailed agenda.
   b. Start the meeting on time.
   c. Move briskly through the agenda. Finish an item, bang the gavel, and start on the next item immediately.
   d. Adjourn the meeting.

2. **What causes meetings to be so long and boring?**
   a. Lack of planning.
   b. Ignorance and indecisiveness of the presider.
   c. Dearth of fair and democratic procedures.
   d. Ill-prepared participants.

3. **How can meetings be shortened?**
   a. See #1,c above.
   b. Limit debate of a motion to the shortest practical time. The chair asks for unanimous consent to limit debate and states the expiration time for debate.
   c. Prepare the following ground rules, and pass them by majority vote. Members may:
      1) speak only after recognition by the chair;
      2) speak only to the chair;
      3) speak only to the motion on the floor;
      4) speak only for two minutes each time the member speaks.

Parliamentarian

1. **Should the chair have a parliamentarian at a meeting?**
   Yes, next to the presider at the head table. Even if the parliamentarian is relatively unskilled, having a team at the head table strengthens the presider, and cools the rash impulses of some members.

Voting

1. **After an election, may someone call for a re-vote?**
   Only if the person elected refuses to run, of if there has been fraud or confusion connected with the election.

2. **May a member ask for the vote received by each member in an election?**
   Yes. The vote for each member should be given to the assembly as a matter of procedure. The thought that someone may have hurt feelings by being defeated must be supplanted by the *necessity* of informing members about *their* business.

3. **Is it proper to vote on the nominating slate as the election slate?**
   No, because members present are not given the opportunity to nominate from the floor, nor to discriminate among candidates in giving or withholding members' votes. To allow the nominating slate automatically to become the election slate substitutes the power of the nominating committee for the power of the assembly.

4. **I know any member may demand a standing vote, but may any member demand a standing *counted* vote?**
   No. Only the assembly may authorize a standing counted vote, a motion that generally requires a majority vote.

5. **Is it better to have a standing counted vote rather than a show of hands?**
   Yes. It is difficult to count a show of hands.

6. **Is there an easy way to determine a 2/3 vote?**
   Yes, double the *negative* votes. If the negative votes are equal, or less than equal, to the positive votes, the motion carries by a 2/3 vote.

7. **May the chair vote only to break a tie?**
   No. The chair, if a member, may vote to create a tie. The chair may not break a tie of a ballot vote.

8. **May the chair create a tie then vote to break the tie?**
   No, because then the chair would have two votes.

9. **The vote is 18 for the motion and 19 against. The chair is *against* the motion. Should the chair vote?**
   No, since the motion is being defeated, which is what the chair wants. The chair votes *only* when its vote changes the outcome of an assembly vote.

10. **When a nominating slate of four nominees for four offices is presented, is a vote necessary?**
    Yes. Each office should be considered separately, giving members an opportunity to nominate from the floor.

11. **If I am present at a meeting, must I vote?**
    No. You may announce your abstention, or just remain silent.

12. **I was at a meeting in which the number of votes cast was less than the number of members present. Was the vote legal?**
    Yes, because no member is *required* to vote. However, if there are more votes than members present, a re-vote must be taken, preferably by ballots distributed to members only.

13. **I was in a group where the ballot vote was tied 15 to 15. One member said, "I didn't vote. I vote for Jim." Jim was declared the winner. Was the chair's decision correct?**
    No. The chair may not sanction a mixed vote, a ballot/voice in this case. How can the chair know the member did *not* cast a ballot? He has only the member's word, and that's not good enough.

14. **As a member at a meeting of my club, I doubted the chair judged correctly between ayes and nays. What could I have done?**
    Simply shout out "Division," requiring the chair to have a standing vote, or stand up quickly and say, "I appeal the decision of the chair. I call for a standing counted vote." If someone seconds your motion and the chair announces the seconded motion, a majority vote requires a standing counted vote. *Then* the motion on the floor is voted on.

15. **Is the negative vote of a motion always taken?**
    Yes, except in the case of personal laudatory motions. One may not inform an ill president his board of directors voted for his early recovery by a vote of five to four.

16. **Is a tie vote a lost vote?**
    Yes, because a majority of the people present and voting did not vote in the affirmative.

17. **What is voting by "acclamation?"**
    The term "acclamation" has no standing. It is better for the chair to take a yes/no vote.

18. **After an election in which the winner did not receive an unanimous vote, should the chair allow a motion to change the vote to make it unanimous?**
    No, because the vote was *not* unanimous. The motion implies the nay voters, having lost, must agree with the majority vote, a pernicious attack on the nay voters.

19. **After lengthy discussion, the motion on the floor was voted on with a voice vote. The chair was not sure which way the vote had gone. What should the chair do?**
    The chair simply says, "The chair is in doubt. Unless there is objection there will be a standing counted vote. The chair sees no objection, so all in favor stand . . ."

20. **I have heard an abstention is a positive vote. Is that true?**
    No. An abstention is a non-vote. However, an abstention favors the prevailing side, whether positive or negative. Abstentions should be used only when there is a conflict of interest, or the member has a possible pecuniary involvement with the motion being voted on.

21. **What happens when there is an adopted motion to have the secretary cast a unanimous vote?**
    The secretary must write out a ballot, sign it, show it to the presider, and keep it with the minutes. Having the chair ask for objections, and finding none, is a unanimous vote.

Nominations

22. **Must nominations from the floor be allowed?**
    Yes, unless bylaws prohibit them.

23. **In our club, all nominations are seconded. Is this wrong?**
    No harm is done if nominations are seconded. It is just not necessary to second nominations, though some members may want to make seconding speeches, nominations being debatable.

24. **A motion was made at our Garden Club. The discussion lasted thirty minutes. A vote was taken; the motion was passed. However, one man who voted against the motion complained the vote was not valid because the motion had not been seconded. Was he right?**
    No, he was wrong. Robert's Rules of Order Newly Revised clearly points out that the discussion by the group serves effectively as a second.

Adjourn

25. May the chair adjourn the meeting?
Yes, with unanimous consent. The chair may say, "There being no other business, and no one has asked for the floor, the meeting is adjourned."

26. May a monthly meeting of a club be adjourned at any time?
Any time a majority of the members want to adjourn it.

27. A lawyer went to court, contending a meeting he attended adjourned while his motion was being debated. Was he right?
No, he was wrong. A member may move for adjournment, another second the motion, and a majority vote, without debate or amendment, adjourns the meeting.

Seconding

28. Must a member be recognized by the chair before seconding a motion?
No. All he has to do is shout out "second."

29. Should the name of the seconder appear in the minutes?
No, because all the seconder is doing is helping to get the motion to the floor.

30. Is there any harm in listing the names of the seconders in the minutes?
No harm at all. If the naming of seconders is an organization's practice, let it continue - until the group changes the practice.

Quorum

31. Is a quorum always a majority of the members?
No, a quorum may be set at any number in the bylaws. Reportedly, the quorum of the 1200-member House of Lords is three.

32. May an organization start a business meeting before a quorum, the number of members required by the bylaws to carry on business, is present?
No, but it can carry on preliminary business, such as opening ceremonies. Call the meeting to order promptly at the appointed hour. As soon as a Quorum is present - have someone counting members as they arrive - start the meeting

33. I was at a meeting where the quorum for the meeting was eight. One person said, "If you bring up that matter, I'll walk out and you'll lose your quorum."
The person was right. If the person walked out, the remaining seven had three choices:
    a) Adjourn the meeting to another time,
    b) Adjourn the meeting, or
    c) Take a recess and try to get an eighth member.

Unanimous Vote

34. May the chair call for a unanimous vote?

Perhaps, but it is more desirable for the chair to say, "If there is no objection to the motion, and the chair sees none, the motion is adopted." If no one objects, the vote is unanimous.

35. Is "acclamation" a unanimous vote?
Since the term is not recognized as a parliamentary procedure, it has no status. As recommended above, #17, it is better to take a yes/no vote - which could be unanimous.

36. May a majority vote be changed to a unanimous vote by vote of the assembly?
No. See #18 above.
"THE CHAIR". . . applies both to the person presiding and to his station in the hall from which he presides." (Robert, p. 21)

37. I get so nervous days before I preside at the Garden Club. I know the rules pretty well, but I'm afraid of hurting people's feelings if I use them too much.
You were selected to run the meeting, so run it. Write out what you have to say, and memorize it - but take it with you. Concentrate on the business to be completed, not personalities. Remember, if you preside briskly and fairly, you will get credit, even from those who would, by their thoughtlessness, disrupt the meeting.

Unruly Members

38. Three people at our monthly meetings carry on a conversation during our monthly meetings. What can I do?
Rise to a point of order, stating, "I can't hear what is being said." The chair should then call for order. If the conversation continues, rise again and say, "I can't hear what's going on because of the conversation being held back here." The chair should have no trouble getting order once more. The chair's responsibility is to keep the attention of the members focused as best it can. But, you must secure your rights by seeing no one takes them from you, and hearing what is going on in a meeting is a fundamental right.

Wording of Motions

39. Must all motions be made according to Robert?
No. Even Robert says the intention of the speaker is paramount, that it is the duty of the chair to help the speaker express clearly what he has in mind. Parliamentary procedure is designed to further the wishes of an individual, or an assembly.

Referring to Committee

40. There is a main motion on the floor. It has been discussed for twenty minutes, and no resolution is in sight. You move to refer to committee, but are told that you are putting two motions on the floor at the same time. Were you right? or Was the chair right?
You were right. Referring to committee is a subsidiary motion to which main motions are subject. Move to refer, have a friend second, then get a vote.

Presiding

41. If I preside, must I use a gavel?
You're not required to use a gavel, and in a small committee meeting, it may be out of place; but in a meeting of twenty or more, it should be used. Practice with a gavel and gavel base before you preside.

42. At the end of a meeting a man complained to me about the way I ran the meeting. What could I do?
Tell him that he had to make any objection at the time of the so-called offense. After the meeting, nothing can be done.

43. I dreaded presiding because I was sure Bill McLaughlin would make his usual ten-minute speech near the end of the meeting, and I didn't know how to stop him. What could I do?
 a) Hold him to the same rules as the other members. (See #3 above.)
 b) Hold to: there is no debate without a motion on the floor.

44. What is meant by the phrase "privilege of the chair?"
There is no such phrase. The term does not exist in recognized parliamentary procedure.

Point of Order

45. At a meeting last week we were about to vote on a question and I wasn't clear what the question was. What should I have done?
Shout out, "Point of order." All business stops while you state your point of order and the chair satisfies it. You, as a member, have a right to know at all times what is going on, and if you're not sure, call out, "Point of order."

Point of Personal Privilege

46. At a meeting a noisy air conditioner unit prevented me from hearing the president. Could I interrupt the meeting to tell the chair about the noisy a/c unit?
Absolutely. You say, "I rise to a question of personal privilege." The chair will ask what your question is, and on hearing it, will call for maintenance help to stop the noise. A point of privilege stops the meeting until the point of privilege is dealt with

Parliamentary Authorities

47. Robert's Rules are so hard to understand. Is there a simpler book?
You may find what you seek among other prominent authorities:

Ray Keesey's, *Modern Parliamentary Procedure*, Houghton Miflin Co., Atlanta, 1974; George Demeter's, *Demeter's Manual of Parliamentary Law and Procedure*, Little, Brown & Co., Boston, 1969; Alice Sturgis', *Sturgis Standard Code of Parliamentary Procedure*, McGraw-Hill Co., New York, 1988; Henry M. Robert's, *Robert's Rules of Order - Newly Revised, 1990 edition*, Scott Foresman, Co., Glenview Illinois; and HyFarwell's, *The Majority Rules* and *Majority Motion-A Pocket Guide*, High Publishers, Pueblo, Colorado are two very practical small books.

CHAPTER II - Chairing with Confidence!

Presiding is difficult because it demands so much: confidence without conceit; poise without pride; firmness without faltering. The presider encourages speakers to express what they may hesitatingly propose, without prejudice for or against what speakers propose.

The presider must manifest an assurance that he knows how the goals of the meeting will be met, and that he will reach them. A little humor may lighten the meeting, but wit is out of place. The presider must take his role seriously, but not react to opposition as if it were personal attack.

Even if overruled by the assembly, the presider must be gracious, accept defeat and disappointment calmly, and go ahead with the meeting. The presider can cry later in private. Personal complaints from the chair are out of order. If the presider cannot take the heat of presiding, let someone else preside.

Leadership always carries with it bumps and bruises. The leader cannot expect to be universally understood, let alone loved by everyone. And presiding is not a favor the presider gives to the assembly. There is presiding to be done, and the presider does it; the presider cannot expect praise, but must be satisfied with an occasional "well done." He will always give more at a meeting than any other single person, will be quietly appreciated by some, and will finish most meetings tired, and somewhat disappointed.

1. Realize you have been selected to run the meeting so, run it.
2. Write out what you plan to say.
3. Expect to be nervous.
4. Offset nervousness by:
    a. Look up questions you have in mind. Write the answers down fully. Take the answers to the meeting.
    b. Practice with the gavel. If you don't have a gavel, get one, and practice with it. Remember you are a means to get club business done, not a person standing in front of your peers.
    c. Determine you will proceed; speak slowly, breathe regularly, and plan what you're going to say before you say it.
    d. Determine to ask for repeat of questions not clearly heard or understood.

Be not too formal, not too informal, but firm and fair. Remember you are a means for the group to get business done. Don't be awed by more experienced members. Use common sense.

If you are not sure of a vote, say, "The chair is in doubt." Then call for a standing counted vote. If you are not sure of a question that arises, say honestly, "The chair is in doubt. Does any member have a suggestion?"

Appoint a parliamentarian. Even if the person is not skillful in parliamentary procedure, the person will help just by being there as your aide and counsel. Remember, the parliamentarian serves you, not the assembly - unless you ask the parliamentarian to speak to the assembly.

The Order of Business

"The Opening"/ Call to Order
Prayer, anthem, pledge, password . . . .

The Business
Approval of the minutes of the last meeting (as read, posted or distributed).
Reports of officers, boards, standing committees, and special committees.
Special orders (specially scheduled business).
Unfinished business.
New business.
Good of the order (Announcements).
The closing
Saluting the colors, secret sign, hymn, announcements . . . (Demeter, p. 14)

"There is no standard rule for including any particular order such as roll call of officers, bills, correspondence . . . Each organization decides for itself what its order of business shall comprise and where to insert the headings." (Demeter, p. 14)

Demeter gives four models of "Order of Business" on pp 20-21 of his manual. From those excellent models any non-legislative organization leader can forge an agenda tailored for the needs of his organization.

Closing The Meeting

When the meeting is over, close it - don't oozle into it. Say, "There being no further business (looking around), the meeting is adjourned."

Be sure you give enough time after your announcement, "There being no further business," count three seconds to yourself before saying, "The meeting is adjourned."

Bang the gavel. Close down the shop. Don't reopen it. Tell anyone who complains to ask the secretary to put the item on the agenda for the next meeting.

Running The Meeting

1. Each member, before speaking, must be recognized by the chair.
2. Each speaker speaks only to the chair.
3. Only one person may speak at a time. No speaker may transfer his time to another member.
4. In debate, each speaker speaks only to the motion.
5. Issues are debated, not personalities or motives
6. In debate, each speaker states whether he favors or opposes the question.
7. There is no discussion without a seconded motion before the assembly.
8. Restrict each speaker to two minutes each time the speaker is recognized by the chair.
9. Always:
    a. Ask for a second for each motion. "Is there a second?"
    b. "The motion to has been made and seconded. Is there any discussion?"
    c. After discussion is over, say, "There being no further discussion, we'll have the vote. All in favor say 'aye.' Those opposed say 'nay.' The 'ayes' have it, the motion is adopted. The next item on the agenda is _____."
    d. Keep the meeting going. Move smoothly from one item to the next.
    e. Expect to make some mistakes. Simply say, "The chair is in error," correct the mistake, and go ahead.
    f. Forget about past errors. You'll make more, you will admit them, then go ahead. Do not dwell on past errors.

Meetings go quickly when chaired efficiently!

When you were persuaded to take the vice presidency two months ago, you were reassured that you would never have to preside because Mary Higgins hasn't missed a meeting for seven years - and she's the president. So, with the fervent hope that you would never be called on to preside, you agreed to take the vice presidency.

Mary Higgins continued to enjoy good health - except this morning, she broke her leg! She would be out of action for weeks, and the monthly meeting of your Garden Club is coming up in a week. What do you do?

Preparing for the Meeting

1. Write out your plan for the meeting, what you want to accomplish.
   a. Confer with like-minded, dedicated people, to modify your plan to make a better plan.

2. Gather information that will offset the opposition you expect to have.
   a. Old Lex objects to anything that costs money. Show how spending money now will save Lex money later.

3. Write out what you will say in difficult moments.
   a. Go to a parliamentary authority, probably Robert's and write out for yourself, "The next item of business is the treasurer's report." After the report is made, read: "The treasurer's report will be filed for audit." Write out every item that you think may cause difficulty. You can always read, but you can't always remember to remember.

4. Go to the meeting determined that you will preside fairly and firmly.
   a. You must not be too strict but you can't be folksy either. Your obligation is to get the business of the Club done fairly and briskly. The pitfall is waiting for each person to be satisfied before proceeding with other items of business. Take the vote, announce the vote, rap the gavel, and in the same breath go on to the next item of business.

5. Set up a written agenda. "An agenda is a list of the specific items under each division of the order that the officers or board plan to present to a meeting." (Sturgis, p. 108)
   a. Follow your usual Garden Club meetings format by distributing the meeting's agenda. At your first meeting, do not innovate with a new format no matter how much you think it is needed.
   b. Discuss the agenda with other officers.
   c. It is the Garden Club agenda. The agenda does not belong to any one individual.

6. Try to determine how long individual items will take.
   a. Say, "There being no objection, the item on paving the driveway will be limited to one-half hour. Each speaker will be limited up to two minutes, and no one may speak twice until all who want to speak have spoken. The secretary will keep track of the time with two kitchen timers." Then, if no one objects, the ground rule is set. If someone objects, take a vote, a majority vote prevailing.

7. Be prepared with gavel and base.
   a. Practice using the gavel before the meeting. During the meeting, be sure to rap the gavel with confidence - even if you do not feel confident.
   b. Practice saying, "The meeting will come to order." Rap the gavel.

c. Practice saying, "The majority has it. The motion is adopted. The next item of business is the Pot Luck Supper on April 7th."

Running the Meeting

1. Run the meeting firmly and fairly.
    a. Read what you have written out. Remember you are a means to get the business of the Garden Club done. Forget that you are an individual.
    b. Immediately point out to gabby people that the meeting is important. You might say, "As soon as the meeting is over, we can all socialize - unless you want a long meeting!" The gabby people will become at least self-conscious, and the peer pressure will probably restrict their selfish chatter.

2. Manifest the confidence that you know what you are doing, where you are going, and how you expect to get there.
    a. Read what you have rehearsed at home in a firm, calm voice, no matter what you feel inside. No successful chairman is always calm inside. However you feel inside, try to show an outward calmness.
    b. Plan how long you expect the meeting to last. Concentrate on the items under consideration, get them voted either up or down, and go on to the next item.
    c. Plan the paths you expect to take to get the Garden Club's business done. If one path doesn't work, use another. There are many roads to Rome. You must not get bogged down in debate over procedures.

Do what you think is right.

The keys to presiding are preparation before the meeting, firmness during the meeting, and a pace that allows expeditious handling of garden club business.

If you think of yourself as a conduit through which the business of the Garden Club is brought to the owners for decisions, you de-personalize the role of chairman - which is precisely what you want to do. You serve as an member of a group that has selected you to preside.

Expect to hear unfair allegations against you. Offset those allegations with facts, pointing out what you have done and why you have done it. Then ask the group, "Is the decision of the chair the decision of this group?"

And after you have presided over a well-run meeting, you will be complimented with, "I'm glad you moved this meeting along. Generally, these meetings take two hours. You did this one in 45 minutes, and everyone got a say." No one will say, "I'd like these meetings to be longer. You moved too fast."

Should someone accuse you of railroading, respond with, "I gave everyone every reasonable opportunity to talk. I noticed you didn't say a word."

"Why should I? It wouldn't do any good."

Then smile and know you have done well. If people are afraid to speak up before their peers, they may not reasonably complain about the meeting later.

Effective chairing assures meeting success!

Cy Manwaring: (protesting) I don't know why you want me to become president. I've only been here for a year, and there must be better qualified people than I am to serve as president.

Frank Knapp: That's just it. There isn't anyone else - anyone we will trust.

Cy: I didn't want to say this, but those monthly meetings are boring, are too long, and those two females, Lila and Dorey, never stop talking. Even if I were elected president, how could I stop them from yakking? If I sat on them, the people who complain about their incessant jabbering would criticize me for being to harsh. And one or both of them would start crying, and I would look like a prize jerk.

Frank: There are ways to eliminate the problem of Lila and Dorey if that's all that's holding you back.

Cy: Easy said. How?

Frank: We will all work with you. You won't have to be alone.

Cy: What about Lila and Dorey?

Two factors are involved: getting the condominium business done, and insuring each owner has an equal opportunity to participate in meetings governed by parliamentary procedure, enforced by a firm chair. How are these lofty sentiments translated into action for this condominium's problem of Lila and Dorey?

It must be recognized that Lila and Dorey irritate more people than Cy, that other people would like for the two to do their socializing outside the meeting. The answer is peer pressure.

Peer pressure skillfully developed and prudently used will tend to isolate these two members who are selfishly ignoring everyone's interest but their own. But how to develop peer pressure!

A Formula for Short Productive Meetings

1. Set up a minimum agenda that will cover the necessary business of the group.

2. Hand out ground rules for the meeting:
   a. Members speak only to the chair. (This will put Lila and Dorey on notice.)
   b. Members must be recognized by the chair. (This will promote order by requiring members to stand to be recognized before they speak.)
   c. Members may not discuss unless there is a motion on the floor. (This requirement will prevent those who want to discuss without committing themselves to a motion.)
   d. Members may speak no more than 3 minutes each time they are recognized by the chair. (This will cause garrulous speakers to hesitate to speak too long. Making them conscious of time that is being measured will prevent many otherwise gabby people from talking too much.)

Implementing the Formula for Short Productive Meetings

1. Practice with a gavel and base at home, saying, "The meeting will come to order." - enough so that your voice becomes clear and confident as you say the words. At the meeting, stand and appear poised as you look around, make eye contact with members then, striking the gavel base loudly and authoritatively once, project confidently the phrase, "The meeting will come to order."

2. If Lila and Dorey continue to talk, stop and stare at them. If they still talk, strike the gavel base <u>once</u> more, and say, "The meeting will come to order." If Lila and Dorey won't obey the rules, say firmly, "If you two ladies are ready, the meeting will begin."

3. During the meeting, if Lila and Dorey, or any other groups hold conversations, stop the meeting and look directly at the offending members until they stop.

4. Move the meeting along briskly. Once an item is voted on, say, "The motion is adopted. The next item of business is . . ." all in the same breath. Remember, if you hesitate, you can expect to lose the attention of some, and will signal others that a little socializing is in order.

Are the above directions too harsh? Must one butt heads with people who are, after all, just being friendly with friends? I am reminded of an auctioneer named Patiky on Long Island who repeatedly rapped for silence in his Saturday afternoon auctions, complaining, "Some of these people start socializing with people they spent the whole morning with." Obviously, these "socializing" people, like Lila and Dorey, were self-centered, and cared too little for serious people who had better use for their time than having it wasted by selfish people.

Of course, it is difficult to correct Lila and Dorey when they are neighbors in a condominium, but one is not correcting Lila and Dorey, per se, one is correcting inconsiderate people who in this case happen to be Lila and Dorey. And the chair can always be sure that if the chair is annoyed by the antics of these persons, other people are annoyed, too, and will welcome the chair's requiring Lila and Dorey to behave themselves. There is no better cure for isolated members in a meeting than to get them involved. It does require tact and considerable butter to get them involved, perhaps, but if they can be involved, it is surprising how quickly they can become supporters of the chair and deport themselves properly in meetings. There is no one quite so opposed to sin as a reformed sinner.

Underlying all effective chairing are:
1. A determination to carry out the responsibilities of chairing, and to implement that determination. (By practicing ahead of time, and writing out a script for oneself, one reduces the near-panic that can accompany the first time one presides, for one can always remember how to read if not how to remember.)

2. Accept the nervousness that accompanies the demanding activity of presiding, live with it, and know that it too will pass away. The sun will rise the next day just as it has for eons of time, despite your personal ordeal.

3. Use common sense. Don't hesitate to laugh - even at your own mistakes. If you make a mistake, fall back on the phrase you memorized before the meeting, "The chair is in error, and thanks Mike for his help." The chair saves face, Mike appears knowledgeable, and the group is reassured by the modesty of the chair.

A layman was asked to preside at a Lutheran church Sunday service - liturgy and sermon. He opened by welcoming people "to the house of God," saying, "You are asked to count the number of mistakes I make. The person who counts the most mistakes will take the service next week."

The greatest personal confidence is predicated on knowing, and knowing you know. The basis for knowledge is study and application. Learning the right phases such as, "The meeting will come to order," and/or "The motion is adopted," "The chair recognizes Bill Bramo," will add measurably to your confidence as chair. If you cannot get a qualified parliamentarian, have a friend act as parliamentarian seated close to you. If you get into a jam, stop and confer with the parliamentarian. If you are still stuck, turn to the speaker and say, "The chair is in doubt. Will you please explain what you are saying."

Chair is Subject to Authority of Members Assembled!

You are sitting at a meeting that has been droning along, and you are beginning to think of the end of the meeting and the long ride home. Suddenly, you hear the president say, "Since I know you all would agree, I have decided to order a new word processor for the office."

You cannot believe your ears. You know the treasury is low, and besides, who is the president to decide on a matter involving hundreds of dollars all by herself? What do you do?

You stand, and say slowly, "I appeal the decision of the chair."

Everyone is shocked into silence. Some look as if they had swallowed something sour; others look at you with amazement that you, as a single member, have challenged the chair. Yet, they should not have been suprised. You are easily within your rights to challenge a decision of the chair. You know the authority for buying something as big as a word processor belongs with the members, not with just the president - and you are right!

The president was stunned and hurt by your challenge. With brimming eyes she looked at you, and said softly, "I was only doing it for the good of our organization."

Nonsense! She was using power she did not have, hoping to convince the members into quietly agreeing with her after the purchase was an accomplished fact.

The president thought, as she said later, that it was a good buy, the office needs a new word processor, and she was saving time by buying it on her own, without going through all the discussion process. It is true that the president would save time by buying it on her own initiative, but she would be spending other people's money without their consent. She was denying the essence of democratic procedure.

The president serves, does not rule. As the Good Book says, "He who would be master of all must be servant to all." The president is there to carry out the expressed wishes of the group she serves, neither to think for the group as if it did not exist, nor to act as though she knew better than the collective judgment of all the other members.

After the president has had her little temper tantrum, you hope that she knows what to do next. She should say, "Is there a second?" Upon hearing the second, she should then provide the reasons justifying what she did. After she speaks, other members may speak, but only once per member. After all who want to speak have spoken, the chair may speak again, and then say, "Is the chair right? If you think the chair did right, vote 'aye.' If you think the chair did wrong, vote 'nay.'"

Since no one else spoke up, you move for a ballot vote by saying, "Madam President, I move that we vote privately on this matter, by writing *yes* or *no* on the blank pieces of paper the secretary will distribute."

The chair then says, hesitatingly, hoping somebody will rescue her, "If nobody objects, that's what we'll do." Nobody objected, the blanks were distributed, written on, and returned to the secretary. The secretary announced that the ruling of the chair had been defeated by a vote of 5 for and 15 against.

The chair is stunned. "But I told them I would buy the word processor!" she protested.

"I'm sorry about your embarrassment," said Mary, immediate past president, "but you should not have made the commitment." Charitably, Mary adds, "I know you meant well, but you did exceed your authority."

You feel terrible, despite the fact that the members agreed with your opinion that the chair had exceeded her authority, and what the president tried to do was wrong. But, if you realize that the president is there to serve all the members, then you can feel better, knowing that you prevented the president from making a mistake, and you saved the organization from spending money it could not afford to spend.

In this case, appeal was an emotional issue. In many cases appealing the decision of the chair is helpful to the chair. Suppose the chair makes a ruling that you feel will be supported by the majority of the members, but will be opposed by a vocal minority, who will criticize the chair. By appealing the decision of the chair, you get a majority vote from the membership - and no minority can successfully argue against the majority vote of the group.

In Orlando, in August, 1991, in convention, the presiding bishop made a ruling, and added, "If you don't agree with my ruling, you can appeal." No one appealed. But the bishop was right. He recognized that the authority for the actions of the convention lay with the delegates to the convention, and he was dedicated to reflect the majority opinion of the delegates, not to impose his own will, nor to imply that he knew better than the combined wisdom of the delegates.

In order to develop confidence in case you need to appeal the ruling of the chair, practice with a friend. You move to appeal, and he seconds; your friend moves to appeal, and you second. Become familiar with the words needed by saying them aloud until they seem "natural" and not strange. You will feel much more in control of your rights by expressing them; and you will feel much diminished if you do not exercise your rights for fear of hurting the feelings of the chair. If the chair's feelings are so tender and so easily bruised, the chair should step aside and allow someone else to serve who can stand the heat and demands of leadership.

The Presider and the Parliamentarian: A Relationship

The principal role of the convention meeting parliamentarian is easily visualized. He sits near the presider, at the head table, and serves as counselor to the chair. Ideally, he speaks only to the chair.

His communication with the presider takes many forms. The parliamentarian writes notes to the presider, pointing out present or anticipated problems: Ruby is running over her allotted time to debate; the assembly's limitation on debate will be completed in two minutes.

Such simple matters are best handled by the passing of notes because the parliamentarian must not be perceived as being too involved in decisions made by the chair, and the chair must not appear to rely on the parliamentarian too much. The chair must avoid referring to the parliamentarian too often for the chair then appears to be weak; and the role of the parliamentarian can be misperceived.

Universally among parliamentary authorities, the role of the convention meeting parliamentarian is to advise and counsel. He is strictly a staff person, having no legal authority in the convention, serving only to help the chair preside more effectively. The chair listens to the advice and counsel of the parliamentarian, but the chair alone decides what will be done. At the same time, the parliamentarian must realize his role, and not become emotionally involved with his advice and counsel. The chair is the person selected to serve the group, and predicates his decisions on a broader base than the recommendations of the parliamentarian. For instance, the parliamentarian may advise the chair that the names of the seconders of motions need not appear in the minutes. From a strict point of view, the parliamentarian is correct! However, if by suddenly changing this long-standing procedure the members become upset, it is better to let the procedure stand than to cause a needless disturbance among the members. Sometimes the parliamentarian needs to rise and speak privately with the presider. The need should be present and urgent for frequent interruption of the meeting while the presider confers with the parliamentarian erodes the position of the presider and artificially augments the status of the parliamentarian.

Most convention parliamentarians have been asked for a ruling during plenary sessions, the presider turning to the parliamentarian, saying, "Let's see what the parliamentarian has to say." Generally, the chair will repeat the parliamentarian's recommendation to the assembly. A challenge to the parliamentarian's recommendation by a member would be fruitless because the parliamentarian has only advisory status in the convention. The ruling made by the chair based on the parliamentarian's recommendation, however, is subject to appeal by any member.

Here it must be emphasized - all five parliamentary authorities researched for this paper agree the parliamentarian makes recommendations; the chair makes rulings.

Preferably weeks previous to a convention, the parliamentarian is provided the constitutional bylaws of the organization to be served, minutes of the previous convention, if available, and other pertinent information that will help him better prepare to serve the presider in the upcoming convention. My most difficult pre-reading of convention-related documents involved an extensive constitution and set of bylaws. Repeatedly each document dealt with the same subject, and frequently came into conflict with each other! I found myself cross-referencing, noting conflicts and contradictions, wondering if I should point them out to the president of the organization.

I fretted over these difficulties until I came to the actual meeting of this 100-person executive board. At the meeting I was placed at the extreme end of the table on the stage, and obviously tolerated only because I was there by constitutional provision. When I pointed out to the vice president who was presiding temporarily, that two contradictory motions had just been passed consecutively, he brushed the matter off.

There must be at least a mutual respect between presider and parliamentarian. If there is also personal rapport, so much the better; but emphasis must be placed on respect. The relationship between the two is a professional one, and too great effort to make it a friendly one can confuse the purpose of the relationship-expediting the business of the organization in a fair and democratic manner.

At one extreme is a cold professional relationship in which both the presider and/or parliamentarian are very conscious of their own turf-and defend it warily. One veteran presider wrote that he had known parliamentarians who were ". . . flustered, disruptive, pompous, and overbearing."

The other extreme is an immediate friendly relationship between presider and parliamentarian. Such an attempt is a poor idea because it confuses the primary reason for the association between presider and parliamentarian.

The best relationship is based upon mutual recognition of the work to be done, and how best to do it. Respect for each other is an excellent basis for a relationship. If friendliness results, fine; but it is not necessary.

Frequently, the parliamentarian regulates the time each speaker uses to ensure he does not exceed the time limitation set by the assembly. At one time I used a three-minute egg timer. Then I found that a person would not talk for three minutes, and I had to wait until the sand accumulated in one end of the timer before I could use it again. Then, I got two egg timers, using the full one while the other accumulated sand in one end. Finally, I got two kitchen timers.

The first kitchen timer beeps when the speaker has completed his two minutes. It is an impersonal way of informing the speaker his time is up. The chair is not involved in the unpleasant chore of telling someone to stop talking - nor is the parliamentarian. And no one can argue very well with a mechanical object that is impersonal, and declares loud and clear to the speaker, "Your time is up."

The second timer is used to inform the chair that a specified time for debate and vote of a <u>subject</u> is up, say, "Ten minutes for discussing dues."

Keeping track of the order of people waiting to speak at three separate microphones in a convention setting is another chore that frequently falls to the parliamentarian. The parliamentarian needs scrap paper. Discarded sheets with typing on one side will do nicely for writing the order of persons at the microphone who wish to speak. For example, two speakers may line up behind microphone #1 before one person lines up behind microphone #2. Obviously, the two people at microphone #1 must be allowed to speak first. But, when there are four microphones in the room, the chore becomes more than a third more difficult. If the correct order of speakers is not carried out by the presider, resentment at the microphones can easily erupt. The parliamentarian may make an honest mistake, but his mistake may not be so interpreted by an angry person speaking on a controversial subject. One solution: have two people keep track of the microphones, the parliamentarian and the secretary.

The wise parliamentarian sets up a teller arrangement before a plenary meeting begins. The teller arrangement must be carefully planned and executed for a good teller arrangement is critical for a smoothly run meeting, and can prevent confusing conflicts at most embarrassing times.

Many of the duties of the convention parliamentarian are mechanical, such as the teller arrangement. Therefore, the parliamentarian needs to see the convention hall well ahead of time, and see to such pedestrian matters as placing large numbers on the microphone so that everyone knows which is #1, #2, #3, and #4.

Finally, between the time the parliamentarian receives the documents he has requested and the convention begins, there must be time for the presider and the parliamentarian to confer. A half-hour seems minimal for a new team. The role of the parliamentarian is many times so poorly known that there can be gear-grinding during the convention before the two persons can develop into an effective team.

An operative relationship can be worked out easily between experienced presiders and parliamentarians. It is the inexperienced, terrified presider who offers the most problems, for he may preside poorly, and he may not know the role of his parliamentarian: he may ask too much of the parliamentarian or he may ask too little. It is in conferring that the two can develop the relationship necessary for the proper handling of the assembly's business.

Offering to help in the follow-up of problems stemming from the convention is a service the prudent parliamentarian offers. Of course, if the follow-up is extensive, there must be an additional fee arrangement. It is rare that the parliamentarian is called upon to act in such office, but the offer builds good will.

Professional fees is another subject. However, to quote Elaine Fulton, executive secretary of the National Association of Parliamentarians, ". . . ten bucks and lunch is not enough." There are guidelines that can ease the embarrassment for the parliamentarian in asking too much or too little, the latter being the greater danger.

Lord Chesterton once said, "I don't take myself seriously, but I take my ideas seriously." Likewise, the parliamentarian must not take himself too seriously, but he must take his work seriously. By separating his persona from his work, he can be content that his expertise helps the assembly reach its goals. In concentrating on the service being rendered he minimizes personal factors that could inhibit his effectiveness as parliamentarian. And, in so concentrating, he fulfills the purpose for which he was retained to help the convention complete its business fairly and democratically.

CHAPTER III - Motions
Conflicting Adopted Motions and a Renewed Motion

Robert states, ". . . no main motion is in order that conflicts with a motion previously adopted at any time and still in force. Unless an adopted main motion specifies a time for the termination of its effect, it continues in force until it is rescinded" (p. 108).

In a meeting of its executive committee of 100 persons, a national organization adopted a motion that stated, "All trainers of organization athletes must speak English." Within an hour, after some discussion of the adopted motion, a motion was adopted that stated, "Only *managers* of organization athletes must speak English."

The parliamentarian pointed out to the presider that the second motion came into conflict with the first. The presider brushed the objection aside, implying that the members would forget the first motion, and remember the second one.

The result of the presider's failure could cause chaos. Those who wanted to eliminate *trainers* who could not speak English could point to the first motion that required trainers to speak English. Those who wanted to eliminate managers who could not speak English could point to the second motion. While it appeared that the Executive Board wanted the second motion, and probably considered the second motion had wiped out the first, such assumption was not warranted. The board had to rescind or reconsider the first motion. The two conflicting motions could not be allowed to stand.

Reconsideration of the first motion would have been easy to bring about. After the discussion that followed the adoption of the first motion had convinced members of the impracticality of requiring trainers to speak English, a person who voted for the first motion could move to reconsider the motion concerning trainers. In making the motion to debate, the speaker can allude to a complication in carrying out the original motion which he can then expand upon during the debate period to reconsider.

During the debate period the speaker can point out that implementing the first motion would wipe out half the trainers for the athletes, thus indicating the need to pass the motion to reconsider, and then to vote down the first motion - the requirement of English for the trainers.

Another procedure that could be used is the motion to rescind (erase, cancel) the first motion by a 2/3 vote, after allowing time for debate and amendment.

At a condominium meeting in Florida a motion was defeated to buy a piece of property because it did not receive the 3/4 vote required by the bylaws. Immediately, proponents for the purchase of the property were seen coercing opponents to the purchase. The motion to purchase the property was then made the sole item for a special meeting to be held later.

At the special meeting, the motion to purchase the piece of property was adopted. Was the second adopted motion legal? Yes, it was legal, being a renewed motion. However, it was tainted in that original opponents of the purchase were allegedly frightened into support for a measure they opposed.

Ethically, the methods used against the original opponents to the purchase are indefensible. While one can easily write from the security of one's workroom that people must stand up for their own rights, and not be coerced, it is rarely easy to act solely from principle. Under the strong pressure from a demanding person, one can be persuaded that one is actually wrong, that the demanding person is right. However, the fault here lies primarily with those who coerce, not with those who are coerced.

From the parliamentary point of view, a motion defeated in one meeting can be renewed in another, a common practice supported by parliamentary authorities. But a corollary of that practice is the expectation that democratic and fair means will be used to bring about renewal of the motion.

Several years ago, the district governor of a New York State women's organization telephoned me, complaining that the national president had decided to change election of delegates to the national convention from district representation to at-large representation. When asked her reason for the change, the president reportedly replied, "The constitution doesn't say I can't do this, so I'm doing it."

A well written constitution or bylaws - they can be synonymous - specify what is authorized for officers and members of the organization. If an action is not authorized, it may not be made on the basis that non-prohibition is the same as permission to take that action.

Not saying no is not the same thing as saying yes.

Sometimes one hears of "the privilege of the chair." The term does not appear in any of the four parliamentary authorities consulted. Strictly speaking, the chair is a single representation of the authority of the assembly, and has, for example, only one vote as other members, and is always subject to overrule by the assembly. The phrase is a handy one - widely used - but like "friendly amendment," it is honored only by practice, not by authority.

Questions and Answers

1. Why can't a group agree simply to ignore the first adopted motion and just use the second one?
Confusion would be created, and doubt would be cast on any decision made by the assembly previous to the current meeting. There are easy ways to correct what the assembly wants to correct: rescind, amend something previously adopted, reconsider.

2. Do you mean that the president, or any other officer, may do nothing unless what he wants to do is spelled out in the constitution or bylaws?
No. It would be impossible to specify the authority and obligations of the president, for example, in detailed form. It is expected that honorable and reasonable people will act honorably and reasonably while in office. For example, if every action that a president of an organization takes must be spelled out before he can take it, the constitution would be voluminous and cluttered with details that could make the document unreadable. It is axiomatic that if too great detail is put into a constitution, specifying what an officer must do, then there is distrust for persons serving in the office, or in a person who previously served in the office. The answer is simple. Specify important requirements of the presidency; for example, elect a good person for the position, and let him function. If he does not function well, dismiss him, or elect someone else the next election.

3. What's wrong with "friendly amendment?"
Who decides if the amendment is "friendly?" The main objection, however, is that the motion which becomes the question when spoken by the chair - belongs to the assembly and not to the original maker of the motion. The only privilege the original maker has is to speak first after the seconding of his motion and the stating of the seconded motion by the chair. This mistaken idea of

the friendly amendment breaks one of the cardinal rules of a properly run meeting: All speakers direct their words to the presider only, not to another member.

4. What should I do if the chair allows a second motion that conflicts with a previously adopted motion?

Appeal the decision of the chair, specifying your reasons. Use a parliamentary inquiry, asking if the two adopted motions are in conflict. Refer to the parliamentary authority, p. 108 of Robert's latest edition.

Double motions are clearly best off as two singles

"Mr. Chairman, I move that we buy a new roof for the club carport, and that it be corrugated steel."

Immediately the chairman should become alert to the problem that the maker of the motion has made two motions: the buying of a new roof, and the composition of that roof. First, there must be discussion of a new roof. Some members may prefer to buy the new roof later, and some may prefer to buy it now. But specifying that the roof be composed of corrugated steel eliminates the discussion of the use of fiberglass and aluminum, to name only two alternative roof materials, and overlooks the possibility that the members may not want to buy a new roof for the carport.

The above motion must be divided into two parts: The purchase of the roof, and the composition of the roof. Example:

Chair: Is there a second to the motion concerning the roof ?

Rolf: I second.

Chair: The Chair points out that there are two motions here: One to buy a new roof for the carport, and the second to require the roof be made of corrugated steel. If there is no objection the Chair will divide the question into two questions. (pause)

Chair: Perceiving no objection, the first question is the composition of the proposed roof. The second question is the purchase of a new roof, composed of materials authorized by the first motion considered. Does everyone understand? (pause) First the materials for the roof, then the roof. If there is no objection-and the Chair sees none-the first question will be the composition of the roof. Is there any discussion?

Art: Mr. Chairman, I know that a fiberglass roof is cheaper, lighter, and more durable than a corrugated steel roof. I move to amend the motion to buy a new roof by striking out the words 'corrugated steel' and inserting the word 'fiberglass' between 'new' and 'roof.'

Chair: Is there a second?

May: Second

Chair: Striking out and inserting is one motion, that is, the membership may not decide to strike out and not insert, or not strike out and insert. You must vote on striking out 'corrugated steel' and inserting 'fiberglass' between 'new' and 'roof' as one motion. Any discussion? If not, are you ready for the question? All in favor of striking out 'corrugated steel' and inserting 'fiberglass' between 'new' and 'roof,' say 'aye.' Those opposed say 'nay.' The motion is adopted.
  The motion before you is to buy a new fiberglass roof for the carport. Any discussion? The Chair, hearing none, asks for those who support the motion to say aye. Those opposed say nay. The ayes have it, the motion is adopted. Without objection, the treasurer will please secure three bids from reputable contractors for a fiberglass roof for the carport and submit the bids at the next regular meeting. The next item of business is . . .

It is obvious that the composition of the roof must be decided first so the voting members can easily understand what kind of roof they are voting for.

Considered the other way around, voting for the roof first, and then the composition of the roof can generate the following discussion:

Member #1: I voted to buy a new roof, but only if it is galvanized. A galvanized roof is the only real choice.

Member #2: When I voted for a new roof, I naturally thought it would be fiberglass, the best, the most modern, and the cheapest to buy.

Member #3: How do you know it is 'best,' 'most modern,' and 'cheapest?' Are you an expert in roofs? I know roofs. Roofs are my business, and fiberglass is not best.

The above questions emphasize the need to vote on the amendment first (fiberglass), and the amended motion (fiberglass roof) second.

Of course, there could be much discussion of the amended motion, and the motion could be defeated because a majority of the members did not want a new roof. However, by carrying on this rather elaborate parliamentary procedure the members had a clear choice to vote the roof up or down.

Other examples of double motions come to mind:

"To commend Member Allan for his new book and to buy five copies for our library;"

"To have a dinner and a dance on July 22nd;"

"To buy a new computer and desk for the office."

Probably the makers of the double motions see their motions as logically connected - and they may be right. But a wiser course is to move for the more important motion - the commendation for the book, the dinner, and the computer first, and each second motion thereafter.

During the discussion the makers of the motions can say, "If this motion is passed, I shall move to: Buy multiple copies; to have a dance following dinner; or to buy a desk for the computer." The speakers thus use "previous notice" to show their intentions. If practical, the Chair should call on members giving previous notice in turn as they announced their intentions, as soon as the pending motion is resolved.

If the members decide not to commend Allan for his book, not to have a dinner, nor to buy a computer, previous notice about the second motions makes no sense. The membership will probably not buy copies of a book it does not commend, not have a dance after voting down the dinner, and not buy a desk after voting down the purchase of a computer.

Any sagacious member who wants a major motion passed will test the temper of the members by discreet inquiries before the meeting to see if there is support for such a motion. Regularly, the Speaker of the House of Representatives of the United States Congress is asked if a motion will pass, and regularly the Speaker will give his opinion. It is the Speaker's obligation to ascertain the probable voting of the House members on important matters.

Testing the waters beforehand also allows the member to build support for his motion, and to learn the size of the probable opposition. Further, he does not necessarily expect to win the first time his motion is presented, knowing that important matters require educating the membership, and talking one-on-one with members, convincing the members that his position is correct, and their votes are needed.

Persuading other members that one's proposal is good for the organization is pivotal to the health and vigor of an organization. Expecting a proposal to pass simply because, in the eyes of the proposer, it is sensible and good, is naive. While one might deplore the ignorance of other members that they cannot see what is obviously right and just, such an attitude counts for naught if one's proposal is defeated. The procedure is simple: The goal is set, and the means to reach the goal are determined. Thereafter, one works hard to secure the votes necessary for the passage of the proposal, counting such effort as necessary and natural.

May a motion be withdrawn?

At a convention of 300 delegates, the chairman of the Credentials committees presented recommendations to the delegates for changing the times of reporting to the delegates the number of people present, and their status.

Chairman: The committee recommends reports of delegates present be made each morning of this three-day convention.

President: You have heard the Credential Committee's recommendation. Is there any discussion?

Delegate Gregor: Mr. President.

President: The chair recognizes Mr. Gregor.

Gregor: We have some important votes coming up, Mr. President. I think we need two reports each day: one in the morning, and one in the afternoon before adjourning for the day.

Chairman: I agree. Let's make the two reports each day.

President (after speaking quietly with the Parliamentarian): The parliamentarian has trouble with changing that arrangement, Bob. Perhaps he will explain for all of us.

Parliamentarian: Under parliamentary procedure, once a motion has been made and announced by the chair, the motion belongs to the assembly, not to the original maker of the motion. Therefore the assembly must give permission for the proposed change.

Delegate Eich: It is not a proper motion anyway. There was no second.

Chair: Functionally, there was a second. When the chairman of the committee makes a recommendation, that recommendation has been seconded by a majority of the committee. In the case of this three-member committee, at least two people have "seconded" the recommendation. The question that must be decided is, will the assembly give permission for the chairman of the Credentials Committee to withdraw his recommendation to have three credentials committee reports, all in the morning. If there is no objection to so allowing the chairman - and the chair sees no objection - the assembly has given unanimous permission for the chairman to withdraw his original recommendation. Mr. Chairman, you have the floor.

Chairman: The Credentials Committee recommends six reports be made, two on each day, one in the morning, and one in the afternoon before adjournment.

President: If there is no objection - and the chair sees no one seeking the floor - the recommendation is accepted.

The above is illustrative only. The chairman should call his committee members together again to see if they agree. However, the purpose here is to show the procedure that protects the assembly from having a motion accepted by it only to have that motion snatched away. If a member objected to allowing the chairman to withdraw his motion, then the chair would ask for a voice vote, expecting to get a majority that way.

Still another route is to have the move for withdrawal come from the floor. If the person moving for withdrawal is the maker of the original motion, and the motion has been stated by the

President, there must be a second to his motion to withdraw the motion. If another person moves to withdraw, there is no need for a second, it being assumed that the original maker of the motion is the seconder.

Demeter (p. 144) asserts that only the proposer of a motion can move to withdraw it, that no second is required. The proposer must withdraw his motion before it has been voiced by the chair, however. Otherwise the assembly must by majority vote grant permission.

The seconder is not consulted on the widely accepted basis that the seconding of a motion is a mechanical process that does not even involve support of the motion by the seconder. In other words, the seconder may simply want to get the motion voted down, and therefore seconds the motion so the motion can be voted on, hoping a negative vote will defeat the motion. Generally, the second and the seconder has so little status that his name does not appear in the minutes.

Sturgis (p. 100) disagrees that a withdrawn motion should not appear in the minutes, stating "A motion that is withdrawn after it has been stated by the presiding officer is recorded in the minutes with a statement that it was withdrawn. No mention is made in the minutes of a motion that is withdrawn before it has been stated to the assembly by the presiding officer."

The obvious recommendation is to know the position taken by the parliamentary authority as stated in your bylaws and stick with that position. If there is doubt about the voice vote to permit the withdrawal of the motion by the objection of one or more members, the doubt should be resolved by a standing vote, the affirmative standing, then sitting, the negative standing, then sitting. If either side shows a commanding lead, there is no need to count the vote.

If there was a doubt about the standing vote, there must be a standing *counted* vote, the affirmative being counted first, then the negative.

There is another aspect to withdrawal of a motion. Suppose a motion made and seconded is withdrawn before repeated by the chair. The maker of the motion may do so, and need not regard the seconder. (Courtesy requires an explanation to the seconder later, privately.)

Of course, there can be a motion from the floor that is withdrawn.

Member Rogers: I move the picnic be held October 15th.

Member Plante: Second.

Member Boyles whispers hastily to Member Rogers.

Member Rogers: Mr. President, I withdraw my motion. I have been told that our usual picnic ground will be closed for the season by October 15th.

The chair has not announced the motion; the motion still belongs to its maker; it has not yet become the "property" of the assembly.

Questions and Answers

1. Why not let the chairman change his recommendation without going through all the parliamentary procedure?

The recommendation is not "his recommendation;" it is the committee's recommendation. Further, the president has presented the recommendation to the assembly, and to allow the chairman to take it back would trample on the rights of the assembly.

2. If no one objects to the chairman's changing the committee's recommendation, is that not an approval of what the chairman has done?

One must not let error go uncorrected. One would allow error to prevail through non-correction of it. Ignoring "small" errors will undoubtedly lead to ignoring bigger ones.

3. Does withdrawal of a motion happen often?

Not to my knowledge. The withdrawal is little known, rarely needed, and presents opportunities for misunderstandings and bruised feelings.

4. Is the motion to withdraw debatable or amendable?

It is neither debatable nor amendable because it is an incidental motion, and incidental motions - with one exception - are neither debatable nor amendable. The reasoning is that debating and amending incidental motions could cause much confusion by debating the *incidental motion*, losing sight of the main motion. It is sobering to think how much confusion and how many headaches can develop from arguing on "how to do" rather than "what to do."

5. Why do you cite so many different parliamentary authorities? Why not simply stick with Robert?

It is true that Robert is used by an estimated 90% of organizations, but some organizations prefer Sturgis, or Demeter. Also, Robert is not Holy Writ. The philosophy of this book is to enlighten and inform, not to promote solely one parliamentary authority's point of view.

Dilatory and Improper Motions

The need for minimal parliamentary procedure for any organization shows itself most forcefully in a meeting where the chair and the other members are butts of the adolescent behavior of a few people. The term adolescent behavior here implies more than one person because one person is usually unable to carry on divisive behavior by himself. Let us be specific.

Connie and Selig come to the monthly meetings to socialize. They will not serve the organization by serving on committees, brushing such responsibilities aside, saying they are too busy for such matters. At meetings they chat constantly with each other, until corrected by the chair. They subside, but are soon chatting again. Worst of all, Selig enjoys making trivial motions. For example, he moved that no more dues be collected. Connie obligingly seconded the motion. What should the chair do?

The chair has two courses. The chair can rule the motion trivial, and not repeat it. The chair's reasoning is that the club cannot continue without dues, and to vote to eliminate dues would eliminate the club. The chair thinks the idea silly, that the majority of club members will agree with him that Selig is just showing off and being contrary.

Of course, Selig can appeal the decision of the chair, and can take even more time while the appeal is presented to the assembly of club members. Selig does not expect to win, but he does love to talk and to have his ideas considered by the assembly - even though he does not consider them seriously himself. Rather he uses them to create chaos.

The chair can repeat the seconded motion to eliminate dues and treat the motion seriously. The debate would surely point out that elimination of dues would eliminate the club, that the motion should be defeated. The motion is presented to the club assembly, and is defeated, only Selig and Connie voting for their original motion.

Meanwhile, time valuable to individual members has been lost. Kevin, who was dragged out by his wife on a good TV night, vows never to attend another meeting of such a stupid organization, Kevin having identified Selig's childishness with the club. Nevertheless, Kevin, a weary commuter who is forced to listen to Selig's nonsense being considered seriously by the chair, has a point.

A chair who refuses to recognize the seconded motion can be charged with "dictatorship" by Selig and Connie especially. If the chair takes Selig's motion seriously, much club time is lost, and many members are irritated.

Demeter (p.58) spurns dilatory motions, saying, "Dilatory motions . . . mischievously or unreasonably obstruct or delay business."

Sturgis (p.91) is even more acidulous in her criticism, writing, ". . . if a motion is outrageously tactless, foolish, unnecessary, or completely unsuitable for consideration, or if it is proposed at an inopportune time, or for the purpose of heckling, delaying, or embarrassing, the presiding officer may rule the motion out of order on his own initiative."

Robert (p.336) is mildest of all, saying, "A motion is dilatory if it seeks to obstruct or thwart the will of the assembly as clearly indicated by the existing parliamentary situation."

All three parliamentary authorities rely upon the firm control of the meeting by the chair; but suppose the chair is weak? Then a member can appeal on the same bases as those given by the parliamentary authorities, thus allowing the assembly to decide the nature of the motions.

Examples of dilatory motions abound: The repeated call for standing counted votes when the vote is clear; constant raising of points of order irrelevant to the business of the assembly; incessant appeals to the decisions of the chair; moving to reconsider and enter on the minutes in order to stop consideration of motions opposed by only two people, motions that would probably be accepted by the assembly; objection to consideration of the question before the assembly on frivolous grounds, to name only a few misused procedures.

As a rule, the chair must be protected from repeated appeals to the chair's decisions particularly when the chair is assailed by pettifoggery, or smart aleck members. Should the chair be so treated by some members - and mistreating the chair inferentially mistreats the assembly - a member can rise to propose curtailing the shenanigans of the irresponsible members by established parliamentary procedure.

The trouble with Selig started long before Selig presented his trivial motion. The trouble started with the failure on the part of the presider to prepare for the meeting properly, to anticipate the negative and obstructionist attitudes of Selig and Connie, and to forestall them. Anticipating and preparing can so arm the chair that Selig and Connie, perceiving the self-assuredness shown by the chair, will hesitate to hamper the deliberations of the club assembly.

The wise chair prepares by thinking: What is the worst that Selig and Connie can do tonight? What members can I call on before the meeting to alert them to possible problems stemming from those two? How can I set up a firm agenda and keep it going? How can I set up ground rules that will offset the mischief of these two particularly?

Then, the chair acts by writing out what he will say by writing down the names of reliable members who will actively cooperate with the chair to promoted the assembly's business and who will share with the chair the responsibility of carrying out business expeditiously, energetically, and democratically.

Improper motions can be made, through ignorance. For example, a member of a not-for-profit organization is forbidden by law from moving to support a political candidate with organization funds. An enthusiastic supporter of the local congressman may move to support the candidate, not knowing the motion is illegal. Others may wish to contribute funds to World Relief, a worthy organization by reputation, but one that should be supported by members as individuals, as they see fit, without involving the combined funds of members of a not-for-profit organization.

A member may make a motion prohibited by the bylaws, or one not authorized by the bylaws. The purchase of large equipment, a tractor, for instance, may be prohibited by a provision in the bylaws. The motion to buy a tractor would, therefore, be an improper motion, but would in no way reflect negatively on a sincere club member.

If the bylaws are silent on the purchase of large equipment, the purchase of such equipment may be outside the purview of the bylaws, and thus unconstitutional. The silence of the bylaws on the purchase of large equipment does not authorize the purchase of the equipment. If the organization has not purchased such equipment in the past, the sudden purchase of it may prove traumatic to the organization's welfare, and to that of the members. A better course would be to insert authorization for the purchase of such equipment in the bylaws - before the equipment is needed.

Some argue that it is better to go ahead and buy the equipment rather than to hold back through some concern for those who may oppose buying such equipment. In the first place, outside those who vocally support or oppose the purchase of the equipment, there is no way of knowing how much support there is in the organization for the equipment. Proposing an amendment to the bylaws would soon show the support for such purchases.

In general, it is better to set authorization for an anticipated action in the assembly into the bylaws before the need arises. Bylaws authorization developed before the possible need for it arises is far better than bylaws authorization developed after the need for it arises. In the latter case, an offended member can charge discrimination, that the bylaw provision was adopted only to prevent the adoption of his motion; whereas, to have the bylaw authorization before a need arises is discriminatory against no one.

Questions and Answers

1. What happens when you have a presiding officer who controls everything and everybody?

First, get other people who agree with your judgment that the chair is arbitrary and non-democratic. Second, all study and practice "appeal, general case," p. 254 in the latest edition of **Robert's Rules**, or in your parliamentary authority. Third, go to the meeting prepared to challenge the chair by appealing decisions of the chair. Four, stick to your guns, and, if necessary, quote your parliamentary authority, from the book, on the floor.

2. How can the chair determine if a motion is frivolous?

The chair can use that charge against a motion in order to control the meeting by cutting off legitimate debate. Members must be aware of their rights, and must fight for them at times. If the chair abuses the authority of the chair by declaring frivolous what you consider legitimate motions, appeal the decision of the chair in conjunction with other people. If necessary, write out what your parliamentary authority says, and read the citation from your paper while holding the floor. It may be better to read than to try to remember, depending upon the strength of your memory and the state of your nerves. The key to achieving your aim is to prepare carefully before the meeting. Improvising your position while standing among people who may be indifferent at best, and hostile at worst, to you, is folly or ignorance. It is hard to imagine a more embarrassed person than a member who challenges an established presider with adequate pre-meeting preparation.

No Motion, No Discussion

"I don't want to make a motion. I just want to discuss our outing."

A similar statement has been made in countless meetings because the speaker does not want to make a motion for any one of several reasons. One may charitably say the speaker does not know how meetings are run properly, or that he does not want to have his name attached to a motion that may fail and thus reflect adversely upon him. A more diverse reason can be the speaker aims to lengthen the meeting, obscuring the procedure in order to enhance his opposition to an anticipated motion. But whatever the reasons, the effective chairman does not allow discussion without a motion for reasons in addition to those presented above.

Member #1: The reason I want to discuss first is I'm not sure we should spend treasury money at this time.

Member #2: Why not? Didn't we budget for this outing as we always do?

Member #1: I don't know, but during these hard times I think we should save the money.

Member #3: There are always hard times. And I don't think these are hard times.

Member #1: You don't think these are hard times? The national unemployment rate is above 6% and you don't think these are hard times?

Member #3: Well, my business is good.

Member #1: Maybe so, but your business is only a small part of the economy. I think we should save the money.

What has happened is the purported debate about an outing has deteriorated into a needless haggle, irrelevant to the business of the organization. After the lengthy discussion is over, no resolution of the outing has been made; and the Chair can expect adverse criticism because the outing was not resolved. The Chair can defend his position by saying, "But people must have opportunity to discuss." And so they must, but only after someone has shown the courage to make a motion.

It is generally assumed that the person making a motion favors the motion. In this case a person opposed to an outing may move it, but he may not speak against his own motion. He may vote against it on the basis that the discussion that followed his making the motion convinced him his motion should be defeated.

The making and/or seconding of a motion does not imply the speaker's support of the motion; it simply shows the person wants to get the motion on the floor for action by the assembly.

In the discussion above, a cardinal rule for good meetings has been broken: Each speaker must speak only to the Chair. Since *ideas*, not personalities, are under discussion, there is no good reason for speaking directly to the maker of a motion and a good reason for not speaking to him. Furthermore, once a motion has been repeated by the chair, and seconded, the motion belongs to the group. The request of one member to another to allow a "friendly amendment" is wrong on two counts: the motion now belongs to the group and every speaker must address the Chair only. If cross conversations are allowed, the meeting is at least protracted in length, and little discernible good can accrue to the other members of the assembly or to the assembly's business.

The *primary* objection to discussion without a pending motion is the lack of a central focal point onto which the assembly can concentrate its thinking. The discussion becomes an amorphous mass that delays and derails assembly business.

In small committees, the rule about discussion is relaxed. Any member, including the chairman - since he may make motions in committee meetings - may want to preface his motion with a *brief* introduction. The danger of having the *discussion* dominate the members' attention is still present. In larger meetings, the chairman must retain control of the meeting by requiring a motion before discussion.

Because committee meetings are generally less formal than assembly meetings, there is a tendency for committees to become lax in procedures. The chairman must resolve that the committee's work will be done by keeping the attention of the committee members directed to the completion of their work.

George: Don't be so formal, Harry. We're all friends here. What's wrong with having some fun while we're working?

Harry: Nothing's wrong with having some fun, but let's have it *after* we've done our work. If we keep horsing around like this, we won't have any time to have fun. I'll tell you what. Let's get the work done by 9:30, and I'll buy the first round of beer at Pat's pub.

Any intelligent industrious person can learn rules about parliamentary procedure. It is the *application* of those rules that is so difficult: not too strict, and not too slack. And the skill in application is another aspect of leadership. It is commendable to learn the rules of parliamentary procedure, but until they are applied in a group situation, they remain an intellectual exercise for the person who learned them. How to lead without going too fast for those who follow is always a central tenet of leadership. The leader who gets too far ahead of those he leads can lose his followers; or, in the case of the military, can get shot in the back.

Negative Motions

A member wanting to obscure understanding and voting by the members, can introduce a negative motion: "I move that we not have an outing this year." The trouble with a negative motion is that a "yes" vote means "no" to the motion, and a "no" vote means "yes." By moving a negative motion, the person voting "no" against not having a motion is voting: "I do not want not to have an outing this year." That is a thicket that is hard to clear, and certainly the voting of some members will be confused.

Chair: A negative motion has been proposed. The Chair asks that the motion be cast in a positive mode. This request by the Chair does not mean the Chair supports or does not support the motion. Those opposed to the motion will have ample opportunity to speak against the motion during the debate time.

One difficulty in casting an unpopular motion in a positive mode is that most motions are passed with more than a minimum majority. Members are accustomed to seeing motions passed. For a member to move what he opposes by offering a positive motion is too big a leap of confidence in parliamentary procedure for most members. To make the matter more complicated, the maker of a motion may not talk against his own motion. Therefore, he should get a like-minded person to move to have the outing, and then hope the other person and others will join with him to defeat the motion.

A bishop once asked a council of a large church if the annual church district convention could be held in the church's large auditorium for the second year running. One member of the Council moved, "I move that we not allow the bishop to hold the annual convention in our church auditorium." The motion was seconded. Then confusion began. After fifteen minutes of discussion, the matter was resolved and the bishop was notified that permission to use the auditorium would be permitted under specific arrangements required by the Council. The clearest reaction to the negative motion was said later, "We don't want no more of them negative motions!"

The Chair must be personally prepared to repeat patiently the proper procedures for expediting the assembly's business. The negative motion creates probably the most confusion in meetings. Someone knows he is opposed to something, and he wants to make sure that the other members *know* he is opposed. However well intentioned the member's negative motion, it must be corrected immediately by the Chair.

Chair: The member has cast his opposition in a negative mode. Would he like to restate his motions?

Member: I said what I wanted to say, and no one is going to make me change it.

Chair: The Chair is not siding with the motion, nor against the motion. The Chair is trying to have the motion presented to the assembly understood by all the members before they vote.

The use of negative thinking and expression can lead to needless confusion:

Member: I think we should have something else besides an outing this year.

Chair: What do you propose?

Member: Oh, I don't know. Anything.

Here again time and energy are wasted because there is no motion on the floor. Requiring motions before discussion requires a member to speak out, and others to voice their views - unless they prefer the price of personal agitation caused by their faintheartedness. Opposition to any proposed action is easy to mount. Reasons, however poor, can be put forth concerning any proposed action. Requiring motions to be presented before discussion cuts down on nay sayers' opportunities to be negative. The Chair must insist that opposition to proposed actions be confined to the discussion period, and an attempt made to balance pros and cons.

There is a popular belief that two negatives make a positive: "She isn't *bad looking*," implies that she is good looking, but does not say she is good looking. The statement is a grudging admission that the female person talked about is not ugly; therefore, she is more pretty than ugly. If that person talking simply says, "She is pretty," there is no doubt about the message conveyed.

The trouble with two negatives in parliamentary procedure is that they do not add up to a positive. "But the bylaws do not say I *can't* call a special meeting; so, I'm going to call one." This attempt to grab power illegally is nicely countered by the axiom that the president of an organization may not on his or her own initiative call a special meeting.

CHAPTER IV -
These thirteen *wrongs* make for thirteen *rights*

WRONG: Wait till the latecomers arrive before starting the meeting. Many people expect a meeting to start late, so they wait till a fashionable time before arriving. The time lag may be five, eight, twelve minutes, whatever time you allow before starting the meeting. Then, when you start, ease into the meeting with informal chit chat about things and people unrelated to the meeting agenda.

RIGHT: Start the meeting promptly at the appointed time. Start the meeting with the pledge of allegiance, or, if that is too formal, start it with introducing new people, or giving information of a general nature. Avoid presenting something substantive that requires a motion from the floor immediately for then the latecomers may become angry, charging you with trying to rush something through. But if you start the meeting at the announced time, the latecomers will suspect they have missed something and will be on time for the next meeting. However, you must be consistent: If you start one meeting on time, start every meeting thereafter on time. You must set a procedure that causes people to want to be present at the start of the meeting, one that also assures them they won't be wasting their time by arriving on time for the meeting.

WRONG: Don't check out the audio visual equiP.M. ent in advance. Expect the volunteer responsible to see that everything is ready. Confidently blow into the mike just before you start the meeting. If the microphone does not work, look aggrieved and put upon, then tell someone - anyone will do - to find the technician.

RIGHT: Before the meeting expect that an electric plug will get knocked out, that a mike won't work, that someone failed to turn the mike on. Find out who the audio visual person is, and talk directly with that person well before the meeting. State specifically what you need and when it will be needed. Be polite, but firm and direct.

WRONG: Since all meeting rooms are alike, it is not necessary to find light switches.

RIGHT: Go around the room with an aide - a delegate or staff person - and find the switches well before the meeting. Then when necessary, tell the aide what needs to be done.

WRONG: Do not collate or staple handout materials. Let the participants pick up one sheet from each pile. This way insures that some people will miss some sheets, and will hold up the meeting while the missing sheets are produced.

RIGHT: See that handouts are duplicated and stapled for each participant, estimating as best you can how many packets of handouts will be needed - then add 10%. There is no participant so self-righteously angry as the late arrival who finds all the handouts gone. Foresee problems as best you can; then act to prevent them.

WRONG: Never set a deadline for a committee to report and never give the committee a strict charge. Committees prefer to work at their own leisurely pace, and they should be able to determine the content of their report and recommendations.

RIGHT: If possible, think carefully before setting up a committee and charging it specifically as to content and time for reporting back to the body that created it. If surprised at a meeting, temporize by declaring the committee will be appointed later, after you have conferred with key people. Then be sure to appoint the committee, with charge and reporting date, before the meeting is over. And hold the committee to its charge and reporting date.

WRONG: If you have an agenda, handle every item, however trivial, during the meeting, even if some people nod and others get restless. Do not postpone items to the next meeting.

RIGHT: Hold over to the next meeting items that can reasonably be held over. Don't be a slave to an agenda if by so doing the business of the organization is poorly served. Forcing people to make important decisions when they are weary and impatient to go is counterproductive.

WRONG: Always "APPROVE" the treasurer's report. Consider any suggestion that the books be audited by a committee to be a charge against the honesty of the treasurer. By approving the treasurer's report you accept financial figures you have not had time to examine and give the treasurer opportunity to use unaudited funds for a weekend at the race track. After all, he might win, and all he is doing is using money to make money - your money.

RIGHT: Accept the treasurer's report by saying, "The report will be filed for audit." When the auditing committee's report is presented, then allow it to be voted on. An audit must not be looked upon as a challenge to the treasurer's honesty; it serves as guarantee that the treasurer is handling organization funds properly, that he has not made an honest mistake, or has not done innocently what is against the law or the rules of the organization.

WRONG: Don't call for the vote when the aye vote is so overwhelming. Calling for the no vote is a waste of time.

RIGHT: Always call for the "no" vote except in case of commendation or organization support. The no vote for a recommendation that the CEO recover rapidly from his operation is worse than ignoring the matter entirely. "The Executive Board hopes for the early and complete recovery of the CEO by a vote of 5 to 4," may be funny, but not to the ailing CEO.

WRONG: React to any criticism of your presiding by standing on "the privilege of the chair." Use sarcasm if anyone challenges you too much, and ridicule any idea that you do not like. Bang your gavel a lot.

RIGHT: Remember, you chair a meeting to help the members decide what to do. The "privilege of the chair" is a myth, perpetuated by strong willed persons who want their own way. Sarcasm is never in order for the chair to use, whatever the provocation from a member. Ridicule likewise is out of place. And banging the gavel a lot is evidence of poor control by the Chair and poor attention by the members. Be willing to have any decision you make subject to the majority vote of the members present and voting. Realize you are a conduit whereby organization business is accomplished, that you occupy an important position, but that fact does not make you personally important. Your function is to serve, not to be served.

WRONG: Re-hash what the speaker has said. Seize the opportunity to take credit for some else's ideas. Expect that your duties as chair require you to repeat what the speaker has said, that otherwise less well endowed people will miss important ideas

RIGHT: Thank the speaker and shut up.

WRONG: Expect the meeting room to be comfortable when you arrive five minutes before the meeting is scheduled to begin. Get angry when the room is too cold or too hot, demanding to know in a loud voice who is responsible for the poor conditions.

RIGHT: Check the day before with the person responsible, or that person's superior. Get to the meeting a half-hour early, and check to see that everything is in order. If you cannot find a reliable member to find the person responsible for the comfort of the room, go yourself. Your responsibility is to see that people deliberate in comfortable surroundings, and you must do all you can to insure the surroundings are comfortable. The members are not interested in giving credit for comfort they have paid for; but they will be loud in their complaints if they do not receive the comfort they expect.

WRONG: Keep the meeting friendly. Allow people to chat among themselves. Don't be a scold, and require people to pay attention to what is happening on the floor. Wonder why you are so tired and unsatisfied after an hour's meeting has taken two and a half hours.

RIGHT: Prepare for the meeting ahead of time. Start it on time. Require that people speak only to the Chair. If people are restless, ask for a recess for ten minutes; then re-start the meeting precisely ten minutes later. Say, "If there is no objection, we will have a recess for ten minutes. We will re-start the meeting at 10:35 exactly." And bang that gavel at 10:35. People will begin to believe you mean what you say.

WRONG: Say what you have to say at least twice because people are not paying attention, and they listen only when you repeat. Don't expect or require them to be attentive because they know they will hear what you say the second or the third time you say it.

RIGHT: Be brisk in presiding. Be sure you have everyone's attention and keep it by moving the meeting along, going from completed item to the next item without pause. Make people want to pay attention, at least out of concern they will miss something important. Break up chatting couples or groups by rapping the gavel, looking at the group, and then saying, "We are conducting important business. We need the attention and input of all members. We want your input."

Prepare for the problems you anticipate, conferring with trusted aides. Discuss problems, not personalities connected with those problems. For instance, don't say, "Old Fred is going to bring up that damned dues business again." Rather, say, "The problem of dues will probably come up again. How should we handle it?"

The good presider believes in direct talk, direct questions with direct answers. However, the effective presider must also know of devices frequently used by uncooperative persons. Specifically, the chair must counter, "I don't think we should give all our money to the Rescue Mission," by saying, "No one is suggesting we give all our money to the Rescue Mission. What has been moved is that we give $25 to the Rescue Mission." This deliberate distraction must be corrected immediately and forcefully.

Another ploy is to so load a motion with amendments that the motion will not pass. If a member moves that $25 also be given to the Salvation Army, and another that $25 be given to World Relief, the members may become so upset that they vote down any contributions.

Still another device is to wrangle over part of the motion in order to defeat the whole motion. The motion to contribute to the St. Vincent de Paul Thrift Shop may be defeated because a member has an anti-Catholic bias. He has a right to his bias, but he should not attempt to impose that bias onto a charitable effort of his organization. To argue against St. Vincent de Paul may be a way of defeating any contribution to any charity.

The chair must "impersonalize" motions, while knowing how personal many motions are. The motions must be addressed, not the authors of the motions. The motions must rise or fall on merit, not sources of origin. The chair is part actor. He must play the role of motivator, sustainer, and arbiter. The role is demanding and those who find it too arduous should simply not serve. But if the Chair prepares and presides well, he will enjoy a unique satisfaction that comes with a job well done - and who knows? Someone else might compliment work well done!

Questions and Answers

1. What's wrong with having the Chair declare a recess without asking the members?

The question arises, why did the Chair not ask the members? If the chair is there to serve the members, it can at least say, "If there is no objection, we will have a recess of 15 minutes, ending at 10:35 when we will resume."

2. How can the Chair cut off a silly person from talking so much?

By asking the person to specify his complaint. For example, if George says, "Everyone here complains so much but no one does anything about it." The Chair can answer with questions: "Does the Board do nothing? Does the President do nothing?" Please tell us exactly what you mean so we can correct anything wrong."

3. Must I have self-doubts before I preside, such as "Will I do well?" "Will people think I'm too bossy?"

Yes. Self doubts are always with the conscientious presider, but they can be controlled. They prevent the presider from becoming self-important and dictatorial. They must not be numbing to the extent one cannot function; but only the person who has not presided thinks presiding is easy. The trick is not to let one's nervousness show, and to reduce that nervousness by pre-preparation and writing out what must be said.

CHAPTER V - The Ordeal of Hilda Hesser

Hilda Hesser was beside herself. She had been persuaded to take the presidency of her 200-unit condominium association in Lake Flowers against her better judgment. She had been assured that she would do fine, and the unit owners would cooperate with her. At her first meeting three lawyers argued with one another about a $500 assessment to be levied against each unit for a new roof. She knew the board had the power to assess, but she hoped to have unit owner support and understanding.

Now, here she was, in the midst of a big fight, and she didn't know what to do.

Hattie: (finally) Will you gentlemen please be seated?

Lawyer #1: No, I won't! I have the floor and I'm not yielding it.

Lawyer #2: You just won't cooperate. You just want to have your own way.

Lawyer #3: We can leave personalities out of this. This is all a matter of law. If you two gentlemen kept abreast of condominium law you would know that in the *Gayoso vs. Little Flowers Condominium* case the court settled the matter once and for all.

Hilda: (pleadingly) Please, gentlemen, we must have order or we will get no place.

Sam Spearson: (growling) That's what those lawyers want. They just don't want to pay an assessment so they're trying to tie this meeting in knots.

Lawyer #1: You're looking for a law suit, Sam. Be careful of what you say.

Sara Farnsworth: (complainingly) We're not getting any place. I move adjournment.

Mary Bean: (her friend) Second.

Chair: All in favor.

The ayes were loud and overwhelming as disgusted people got up and started to leave. Poor Hilda had no opportunity to ask for a no vote.

Later, Hilda sat in her condo unit and wept. What went wrong? What could I have done? Why are those lawyers so mean? Why did I take this stupid job in the first place?

Let's consider what Hilda could have done before the meeting.

First, she had to realize that the $500 assessment would cause a ruckus; so, previous to the meeting, she should have:

1. Set up a written agenda, listing the topics to be covered. Plan to distribute the agenda to the unit owners present at the meeting.

   2. Set up written "ground rules" to be distributed at the meeting:
      a. No one speaks until recognized by the chair;
      b. Every speaker must speak only to the chair;
      c. No dialogue between members is allowed;

d. No discussion without a motion on the floor;
e. No members may speak more than two minutes at any one time.

3. Secure the services of a qualified parliamentarian, and work with the parliamentarian before the meeting. Introduce the parliamentarian to the group at the beginning of the meeting.

4. At the meeting, immediately distribute the "ground rules" and say, "If there is no objection these are the rules for tonight's meeting. The chair, hearing no objection, declares these rules in effect."

Hilda must now resolve that she will control the flow of the meeting's business. She must work with the parliamentarian as a team, recognizing that the parliamentarian is her counsel, and works to support her.

She knows the parliamentarian speaks to the group only as she allows the parliamentarian to speak, that the parliamentarian is neither super boss, top sergeant, nor court of appeal. She knows what the chair says holds until and if overruled by the assembly, and the parliamentarian will help her in procedures throughout the meeting.

She must be ready to correct vigorously and courageously the first speaker who breaks any of the meeting rules. Ideally, she would have practiced with her parliamentarian and a couple of close friends before the meeting, testing all the disruptions she and the friends can imagine that could upset the owners' deliberations. Then at the meeting she would have been ready for the onslaughts of pettifogging attorneys.

She must consider the worst possible scenarios: The three lawyers have agreed among themselves to block the proposed assessment by disrupting the meeting so the unit owners will become disgusted and go home. The lawyers would then have won the day: no assessment would be authorized.

Consider Hilda's course of action to offset what she suspects may happen. She must carefully preplan the meeting, work out what she must do, and the order of the doing. She may want to write out what she's sure she must say before the meeting begins so that no matter the turmoil of the meeting, she can still function by reading what must be done.

By distributing meeting rules and asking the assembly to adopt them, she sets up peer pressure support. If the unit owners understand that everyone is bound by the same rules, some will tell the lawyers to abide by the rules ("shut up and sit down"), and the lawyers' devious delay will be eliminated, thereby protecting the rights of the other condo owners.

The chair cannot offset a plan for organized chaos by the three lawyers with pious hopes for fair play. If ". . . the future belongs to those who plan for it," then the chair must plan carefully - and carry out those plans. What must be recognized is the inherent human determination to control. Either the chair controls the meeting, or the lawyers will control it by destroying it.

Hilda must determine to serve the assembly, even if by so doing she must offset unpleasant and self-centered, professionally trained individuals. As chair, Hilda must be firm first, then pleasant if she can be. She is there to conduct the business of the owners, and she must use necessary and legitimate means to conduct the owners' business. Being popular is not synonymous with being effective. Hilda must opt to be effective. She can then enjoy popularity - if it comes her way.

The presence of a qualified parliamentarian has a sobering effect on those people who would exploit what they perceive to be the chair's reluctance to confront disruptive members; and disruptive members must be confronted so business can be accomplished.

What Hilda failed to realize were her obligations as president, no matter the assurance from others that her presidency would go smoothly. They could no more read the future than could Hilda; and expecting human organizations to run smoothly is naive.

Once Hilda accepted the presidency, she was as much involved as if she had campaigned for the job. Her obligation is like pregnancy - there's no such thing as being slightly pregnant.

One does not preside expecting other people to agree, or even be agreeable. One presides knowing business must be carried out, and that parliamentary procedures will be helpful, but they are not substitutes for pre-meeting preparation and personal courage. Hilda must concentrate on what must be done, offsetting fear of negative reactions by setting a positive course.

There is the fable of a man who rode his small donkey while his son walked alongside. When criticized by people for riding while his son walked, he swapped places with his son. Then the son was criticized for riding while his father walked. So both men got on the donkey. Then they were criticized for overloading the donkey. So neither rode, but got a long pole and carried the donkey. People criticized them for carrying the donkey. They realized the donkey was heavy; so when they came to a river, they threw the donkey into the river, causing the donkey to drown.

The moral of the story: if one tries to please everyone, one pleases nobody.

Hilda's goal must be clear: The accomplishment of business. She must ignore the flea bites of unreasonable people who can criticize far better than they can chair, and do what she was selected to do. She may bend in procedure - if that is the will of the group - but she must remain firm in her determination to accomplish her goals. The price? Nervousness, unsureness, loss of sleep, and self-criticism for taking the job in the first place.

Charlie's Meeting, Charlie's Rules

Charlie Raddick: All right, you guys, sit down and shut up. It's time to start the meeting. (banging the gavel loudly several times.)

The members kept talking and laughing and ignoring Charlie at the regular monthly meeting of Poker Pals, a group of thirty men who play poker every Thursday in a rental room in the American Legion Hall.

Charlie became even angrier as he repeatedly banged the gavel, becoming more and more annoyed the more the twenty-nine other members ignored him.

Charlie: Damn it, sit down and shut up, or I'm leaving!

Max: Don't get your bowels in an uproar. (As he slowly disengaged himself from a group of four noisy men, and just as slowly sat down.) This ain't the United Nations and you ain't the Secretary General.

Leisurely, the other members finished off conversations, sat down, and reluctantly faced Charlie.

Charlie: We've got lots of work to do, so let's get started.

Max: Don't act so important, Charlie. What's so important that you've got to act like the great dictator? Lighten up, you'll have a stroke.

Ignoring Max, Charlie ran through his three-item agenda: minutes, old business, new business and adjournment. Throughout the meeting there was the constant buzz of conversations taking place all over the floor.

Max: (whispering to his friend, Frank) We need a new president, Joe. Charlie is getting a big head.

Frank: You want to be president, Max?

Max: I'll kick your butt if you nominate me. I don't want that stupid job. Nobody has any respect for the president anyway. Who wants to try to control these jokers? This club would be OK if Charlie didn't try to boss everybody.

Charlie: Any more new business?

Max: Adjourn.

Charlie: Affirmative vote? (He got a loud 'yea' response. He didn't bother with the negative vote.)

Max: Let's play poker. We've had enough of that stupid business meeting.

What was wrong?

Charlie used a piece of wood to establish his authority. The gavel, shaped like a weapon, was used to establish the position of the chair, threatening twenty-eight men who ignored the sound until they were ready to start business.

"Sit down and shut up,' irritated the members to the extent it had any effect at all. The phrase is insulting and belittling. It started the meeting on a tone of bluster and abuse.

Threatening to leave if he does not have his way is poor procedure on Charlie's part. No presider can take on twenty-eight non-cooperative members and expect to win. There is here an overtone of "I'll take my ball and go home," as empty a threat here as during childhood.

Max represents the worst in member participation; he is rude, crude, uncooperative, non-productive, a thoroughly negative member. He needs curbing.

Shouting out "adjourn" reflects the poor quality of the meeting. Accepting such behavior promises unsatisfactory future meetings. Finally, Max's negative comment,". . . that stupid meeting business," demeans the importance of necessary decisions the members must make.

What to do?

Institute ground rules:
(a) A member must be recognized by the chair before speaking.
(b) The speaker speaks only to the chair.
(c) There is no discussion without a motion on the floor.
(d) No member speaks more than two minutes at a time.
(e) No personal attacks may be made on any other member.

There must be a reasonable respect for the club itself. If the club is viewed contemptuously - as Max views it - the club will suffer. Until moderate standards of member conduct and presider attitudes are established, the club will lurch along to the dissatisfaction of all its members.

The Cookeville Birdwatchers' Society

It is the monthly meeting of the Cookeville Birdwatchers' Society. The meeting is being held at the society's clubhouse. President Pitt is presiding. The time is 8 p.m., April 23, 1997.

President: It is now 8 o'clock. There being a quorum present, the meeting will come to order. (raps the gavel) The minutes of the last meeting have been distributed. Is there anyone who has not received a copy of the minutes? (pause) Are there any additions or corrections to the minutes? The chair, hearing none (pause) declares the minutes adopted as presented. Is the treasurer ready to make a report?

Treasurer: The treasurer is happy to report that the balance in the checking account is $154.15, with no outstanding bills unpaid. The balance in the savings account is $450.35, including interest paid by the bank into account on April 1st of $5.03.

President: Without objection, the treasurer's report will be filed for audit. (raps gavel) The next order of business is the consideration of the dinner-dance. The assembly will recall that the dinner-dance was under consideration at the last meeting, but that time did not allow a decision concerning the dinner-dance. The dinner-dance is now brought up as unfinished business.

Member A: Mr. President:

President: The chair recognizes Member A.

Member A: Mr. President, I move that the Cookeville Birdwatchers' Society have a dinner-dance on June 23, 1997 at Rose's Restaurant.

Member B: Second.

President: It has been moved and seconded that the Cookeville Birdwatchers' Society have a dinner-dance on June 22, 1997 at Rose's Restaurant.

Member C: Point of order, Mr. President. I believe that date was June 23rd, 1997 not June 22, 1997.

President: Thank you, Member C. The chair stands corrected. The proposed date for the dinner-dance is June 23rd, 1997. Is there any discussion?

Member D: Mr. President.

President: The chair recognizes Member D.

Member D: I move to amend the motion by including the phrase, "starting with a cocktail hour at 7 p.m., then having the dinner start at 8 p.m."

Member E: Second.

President: You have heard the proposed amendment to the motion on the floor. Member D. moves that the phrase, "starting with cocktail hour at 7 p.m., then having a dinner starting at 8 p.m." be added to the motion on the floor. Is there discussion on the amendment?

Member F: Mr. President.

President: The chair recognizes Member F.

Member F: Mr. President. May I amend the amendment?

President: Yes, you may. There is a motion on the floor, with a primary amendment. The motion may also have a secondary amendment. If the secondary amendment is also seconded, then the assembly will act on the secondary amendment first, and then the primary amendment, then the motion on the floor. Does everyone understand what the procedure is? What is the amendment you propose, Member F?

Member F: Mr. President, I move to amend the motion by adding the phrase, "to be ended by 12:00 P.M.

Member E: Second.

President: The motion has been moved and seconded. The amendment that the assembly must consider is the secondary amendment, "to be ended by 12:00 P.M." The assembly is voting only on the secondary amendment at this time. Is there any discussion? (pause) There being no discussion, all those in favor of the secondary amendment," to be ended by 12 P.M. " will please say "aye." Those opposed will say "nay." The "ayes" have it, the secondary amendment is adopted. The assembly will now consider the primary amendment. Will the secretary please read the primary amendment?

Secretary: The primary amendment reads, "starting with the cocktail hour at 7 p.m. and then having a dinner starting at 8 p.m."

President: You have heard the primary amendment so that if the motion is adopted it will read, that "The Cookeville Birdwatchers' Society have a dinner-dance on June 23, 1997 at Rose's Restaurant, starting with a cocktail hour at 7 p.m. and then having the dinner start at 8 p.m., to be ended by 12:00 p.m. The assembly is voting on the primary amendment, "starting with a cocktail hour at 7 p.m. and then a dinner at 8 p.m." Those in favor of the primary amendment say "aye." Those opposed say "nay." The "ayes" have it. The primary amendment is adopted. The assembly will now vote on the amended motion. The secretary will please read the motion as amended.

Secretary: (Reads amended motion).

President: All those in favor of the motion as amended will say "aye." Those opposed will say "nay." The "ayes" have it. The motion is adopted. The Cookeville Birdwatchers' Society will have a dinner-dance on June 23, 1997 at Rose's Restaurant, beginning with a cocktail hour at 7 p.m., and then a dinner at 8 p.m., to be ended by 12: 00 p.m. (Raps gavel.)

It is obvious that more can be done to this motion. The matter of "dance" was not mentioned in any of the amendments. The time limitation on the dance could have been specified. The reason for not including these items was the length of the motion with the amendments.

President: The next item of business is the matter of dues.

Member G: Mr. President.

President: The chair recognizes Member G.

Member G: Mr. President. I move that the matter of dues be referred to a committee, and that 10% of the dues go to the building fund.

Member H: Second.

President: You have heard the motion, which has been seconded. Without objection (pause), the chair will split the pending motion into two motions: setting up a committee to consider dues, and a motion to allocate 10% of the dues to the building fund. Without objection (pause), the matter of dues will be referred to a three-person committee, composed of Members Able, Baker, Charles.

The next motion to be considered is allocating 10% of the dues. Is there any discussion? There being no discussion (pause), are you ready for the question? All in favor say "aye." Those opposed say "nay." The motion is adopted. Without objection, any change in dues will take effect January 1, 1998 (raps the gavel). The next item of business is the matter of the annual convention.

Member M: Mr. President.

President: The chair recognize Member M.

Member M: Mr. President. In light of the large amount of business that this organization has accomplished today, and the complexity of planning for the convention, I move that the consideration of the convention be postponed till the June meeting.

Member N: Second.

President: You have heard the motion. Is there any discussion?

President: There are several members who want to speak. Since the motion was made by Member M., he has the right to speak first.

Member M: The reason that I ask for the postponement, Mr. President, is that between now and the next meeting I will provide materials that were developed for past conventions. I will have the materials ready for the next meeting. I urge the assembly to postpone the matter of the convention until the June meeting.

President: Is there further discussion? The chair, without objection, rules that the matter of the convention is postponed till the June meeting.

Member P: I appeal the ruling of the chair.

Member Q: Second.

President: The ruling of the chair has been appealed. The motion is debatable but not amendable. Is there further discussion? There being none, the question will now be put. Shall the decision of the chair stand as the decision of the assembly? Those in favor say "aye." Those opposed say "nay." The decision of the chair is upheld, the matter of the convention is postponed till the June meeting. (raps gavel)

Member R: Mr. President.

President: The chair recognizes Member R.

Member R: The next item of business is listed as being changing the name of this organization. I move that this item be tabled.

Member S: Second.

President: It has been moved and seconded that the matter of the changing of the name of this organization be tabled. This motion is neither debatable nor amendable. All those in favor of tabling the motion say "aye." Those opposed say "nay." The "ayes" have it. The motion is tabled. Is there any unfinished business?

Member T: Mr. President.

President: The chair recognizes Member T.

Member T: We have talked a lot about buying a new sign for the rusty old sign that we now have. I move that we buy a new sign to replace the present rusty sign in front of the clubhouse.

Member G: Second.

President: You have heard the motion to replace the sign now in front of the clubhouse with a new sign. Is there any discussion? There being no discussion, are you ready for the question? All in favor say "aye." Those opposed say "nay." The motion is adopted. The sign will be replaced. There is money in the budget for the replacement. Will the secretary please see to the replacement of the sign?

Member U: I move to take the item about changing the name of the organization from the table.

Member R: Mr. President. That item of business has been settled. Member U cannot bring it up again in this same meeting.

President: The chair rules that Member U. does indeed have the right to move to take the item that was tabled from the table because substantial business has taken place since the tabling of the item. Is there a second?

Member V: Second.

President: The motion to take from the table is just the reverse of the motion to lay on the table. That is, neither debatable nor amendable. Those in favor of taking the motion from the table say "aye." Those opposed, say "nay." The "nays" have it. The motion to take from the table is defeated. Is there any new business?

Member L: Mr. President.

President: The chair recognizes Member L.

President: Mr. President. I move to reconsider the motion to buy a new sign for the clubhouse.

Member X: Second.

President: Did Member L. vote with the prevailing side, that is, did Member L. vote for the purchase of the new sign for the clubhouse?

Member L: Certainly not. It was not a good idea then, and it is not a good idea now.

President: Under the rules of parliamentary procedure, you may not move to reconsider a motion for which you were not on the prevailing side. The chair rules your motion out of order. (raps gavel) Is there any new business? (pause) There being no new business (pause) the meeting is adjourned.

OR

Is there any new business?

Member W: I move adjournment, Mr. President.

Member Y: Second.

President: It has been moved and seconded that the meeting be adjourned. All in favor say "aye." Those opposed say "nay." The "ayes" have it.

Member Z: Mr. President.

President: The chair recognizes Member Z.

Member Z: Mr. President, I wish to inform the members that contributions to the bird sanctuary fund are going along nicely. We have collected over $300 this year.

President: The meeting is adjourned. (raps the gavel)

George was Sharp

George Washington was not only a good politician, he was an alert parliamentarian. In 1787 at the Constitutional Convention in Philadelphia, a motion was made "that the standing army be restricted to 5,000 men at any one time." Since Washington, as presiding officer, could not offer a motion, he turned to another member and whispered: "Amend the motion to provide that no foreign nation-enemy shall invade this country with more than 3,000 troops."

from *Successful Meetings Magazine*

UNFOCUSED Meetings Destroy an Organization

"When Dora debates a motion," Lorraine told her friend, Erica, 'I can't tell whether she's **for** the motion or **against** it." The Chair is probably equally confused. How does the Chair keep the discussion on track?

First, each person speaking must be required to make one of two statements: "I speak **for** the motion," or "I speak **against** the motion." The Doras of meetings frequently speak from indecision, and their words reflect too accurately that indecision. Dora does not think clearly before she speaks, and hopes talking aloud will clarify her thinking. It rarely does.

Meanwhile, the meeting is protracted, more heat than light is generated, and a smoldering resentment against Dora develops. Perhaps Dora means well, but her good intentions are poor excuses for jumbled thinking and rambling verbal expression.

The Chair, keeping in mind its obligation to be tactful, may hesitate to interrupt Dora's meandering because he does not want to offend Dora. However, the Chair's greater obligation is to expedite the business of the meeting, while letting Dora down as gently as he can. "The Chair does not understand what you are saying, Dora. Will you please tell the Chair whether you are speaking in favor or against the motion on the floor?" Of course, Dora can become offended; but if she does, she should 1) not speak in meetings, or 2) get her own thoughts straight before speaking out.

Requiring speakers to declare their positions on the question before the assembly can be done in a less personal, more effective way by the assembly's agreeing upon ground rules before the substantive part of the meeting begins. By typing up and distributing rules requiring speakers to address only the Chair, to take turns, and to be recognized by the Chair, one sets the necessary restrictions and ambiance for the meeting. To those necessary requirements can be added, "Each speaker must declare whether he is speaking for or against the motion on the floor."

Written ground rules focus the attention of the Chair and the members on rules that govern the actions of everyone; and those rules create a peer pressure that eases the burden of the Chair in running a good meeting, precluding unfocused meetings that are deadly to the vigor of an organization.

There is a careful distinction between the Chair's saying, "You are out of order," and "What you are saying is out of order," or more tactfully, "We can't discuss that right now. Maybe you will want to bring that up after we have resolved this motion."

In a club meeting in New York that dealt with the selling and buying of club property, one member - a clone of Grandma Moses - kept talking about the history of the club at a time when the motion on the floor was the selling of the club. The Chair repeatedly told the older lady, "You are out of order," meaning, "What you are saying is out of order," but the lady serenely sailed on, ignoring the rapping of the gavel, just waiting until it stopped interrupting her so she could continue to talk about history that was patently important only to her. Certainly, what she had to say was out of order but like Grandma Moses, she was not easily dissuaded.

Restricting speakers to two-minutes time slots can also militate against the speakers who are mesmerized by the sound of their own voices and seduced by the sterling quality of their own thinking. Precluding speakers' misuse of the debating process **before** abuses arise is both practical and ego-protecting for the undisciplined debater.

The Chair must allow and encourage reasonable and germane debate. Even if the Chair is correct in its ruling that the speaker is not speaking to the motion before the assembly, the Chair's ruling may appear arbitrary and unfair to the other members. If unsure how to rule, the Chair can say, "The Chair is unsure if the member is speaking directly to the motion before the assembly. All those in favor of allowing the speaker to continue, say "aye." Those opposed, say "nay." The Chair can secure a decision from the majority of the members, and can act, voicing the authority of the assembly wherein lies final local authority. More practically, the Chair can try to redirect the speaker into proper debate by **asking**, "Do you mean . . .?"

Chair: You have heard the motion to have a tailgate party before the game. Is there any discussion?

Tony: I think the tailgate party is dumb. Let's have a picnic instead.

Chair: The Chair understands you are opposed to the tailgate party.

Tony: You bet I am. What do you think I just said?

Chair: The Chair must rule your suggestion about the picnic out of order because it is not germane to the motion on the floor.

Tony: Of course it is. You're just trying to be bossy.

Chair: The Chair will overlook your intemperate language, Tony. What the Chair is trying to point out is suggesting a picnic as part of the discussion of the tailgate party is out of order If you want to move to **substitute** picnic for tailgate party, that can be done.

Tony: You're trying to make this whole business complicated. Just ask for all those who are in favor of the picnic to raise their hands. If there is a majority, there is no need to vote on the tailgate party.

Chair: The meeting will follow the proper procedures as required by our bylaws. No member may decide to substitute his own rules for the established rules of our club. The Chair repeats: the member may either move to substitute the picnic for the tailgate party, or may speak against the tailgate party. If the tailgate party is defeated, then the member - who will be recognized first by the Chair - may then make his motion about the picnic.

Tony's actions and attitudes endorse most convincingly the need for faithful adherence to parliamentary procedure. It is clear that Tony wants his own way, and is impatient with anything or anyone he perceives as stopping him. For instance, Tony wants no debate on his demand for a picnic. He demands an immediate vote. He does not want discussion; he just wants to have his own way.

Within all the members is the desire to have their own way. It is a microcosmic example of the continuing conflict between self and society: I want what I want when I want it, and the people who stop me are my enemies. Yet the individual must necessarily curtail his individual choices for the good of the group. There is strength in the group, but that strength is based on individuals willing to curb individual rights for group rights. Tony could think in terms no greater than the immediate satisfaction of his own greed.

A speaker may speak unrelated to the motion on the floor:
inadvertently (he thought he was speaking to the point);
selfishly (I've got a better idea);

maliciously (I'll wear these people down and get what I want when they finally give up), or **ignorantly** (I don't know why we need all these stupid rules about discussing).

The speaker who is out of order because he has not been recognized by the chair can be out of order for several reasons:
1) The person thought he had been recognized by the Chair;
2) The person was so determined to speak that he pushed ahead of other people;
3) The person started speaking because he thought he was next to speak.

Concerning discussion on the floor, the Chair must be analytical but not judgmental; that is, the Chair must recognize **what** members propose, but ignore possible reasons members propose what they do. The Chair must preside, not pry. The adage, "Your actions speak so loud I can't hear your words," applies here. The Chair must be calm, firm, fair, and determined to see the club's business managed according to club procedures. The Doras and the Tonys of organizations must be managed firmly and fairly, without fear or favor.

All members must operate within the restrictive framework of procedures for the good of all. Otherwise, a club would be a gathering of individual human beings, all talking at once, each doing his own thing, with no chance of concerted action for the good of all. On one side is the chaos of extreme individuality, on the other side is oppression by the group; in the middle is the route of parliamentary procedure that protects the rights of the individual and the group, thus making progress possible.

Questions and Answers

1. What's so magic about two-minutes per speaker?
Nothing, but my experience has shown it to be most effective. Timing a speaker is like drinking martinis -one's not enough and three's too many.

2. How can the Chair stop a person from talking too long?
By distributing ground rules at the beginning of a regular meeting, having those rules adopted by majority or unanimous consent ("If no one objects, the rules are adopted.") and then referring to the adopted rules as situations require.

3. Do you recommend a time limitation for discussion of a subject as well as a time limitation for each speaker?
Yes. Discussion of a seconded motion that exceeds a half-hour causes me to suspect that the matter may (1) need referring to a committee, or (2) may need to be postponed to the next regular meeting, or (3) may be the sole subject for a special meeting. Setting a time limit focuses the discussion and persuades the garrulous speaker to concentrate his thinking and his speaking.

CHAPTER VI - Subsidiary Motions
An Overview

What happens when somebody makes a motion? A number of things, but there are seven motions that will get most presiding officers through the rough waters of most meetings. These motions, called subsidiary motions, treat solely with the main motion on the floor. Some of them are familiar, some are rarely used; but knowing about them is vital to successful presiding officers. There is a precedence in these motions shown by the following chart. It must be kept in mind that the higher the motion, the more senior it is. It overrules any motions under it. Further, the movement of precedence, or seniority, goes upward, starting with the main motion.

Precedence of motions

7. Lay on the table
6. Call the previous (pending) question
5. Limit or extend debate
4. Postpone to a definite time
3. Refer to a committee
2. Amend
1. Postpone indefinitely

First, *postpone indefinitely*, is rarely used because it is little known and even less understood. For instance, Mrs. Carpenter moves a main motion to buy a typewriter for the secretary. The motion is seconded and announced by the chair.

What can happen to that main motion?

If the motion to postpone indefinitely is passed, the main motion is killed for that meeting. This motion is used when the motion on the floor is unpopular, or possibly embarrassing. A majority of the people present have to agree to postpone indefinitely.

Second, the main motion may *be amended*. A member may add, insert, delete, or delete and insert words or phrases that will make the main motion acceptable to the majority of the members present and voting.

Third, the motion may be referred to a committee. That committee may be voted in by the assembly, be appointed by the executive board, nominated by the chair and voted on by the assembly, or selected by the chair. The first is the most democratic, the fourth is the least democratic. But, there are good reasons for each process/method.

For an assembly wrangling for an hour over a matter for which the assembly lacked adequate information, the appointment of a committee would allow the amassing of needed information so that the assembly can make its decision.

Fourth, *postpone to a definite time*, actually, no later than the next regular meeting.

The chair for instance, promises to provide additional information about a zoning regulation at the next meeting. The motion could come from the chair as, "There being no objection, the matter will be placed as an item on the agenda for our next meeting." Or a member can say, "I move that the matter of the zoning regulation be placed on the agenda for the next meeting," followed by a second and a majority vote. Once placed, the item must be considered at an appropriate time at the next meeting, unfinished business being a particularly appropriate place.

Fifth, *limit or extend debate*. Limitations can be set easily in anticipation of a lengthy debate. One proven procedure is to have the assembly agree to limitations, such as: one half hour for debate of the motion, each person speaking being limited to two minutes, no person to speak twice until everyone who wants to speak has spoken. Extension of debate may be authorized by a 2/3 vote of the assembly. Such time must be strictly monitored and the limitation honored.

Sixth, *the previous question* "Previous" means "pending" in this case. A member, thinking debate has gone on long enough moves the previous question. The motion, seconded and announced by the chair means that 2/3 of the members present and voting must authorize cessation of debate and an immediate vote. Since a 2/3 vote is required, care must be taken that the vote is either a standing vote or by a show of hands, if the assembly is under thirty. Having tellers count and double check the vote as necessary.

After the vote to stop debate and vote has been accepted by the assembly, then the immediately pending motion must be voted on. Agreeing to stop debate and vote is a separate issue from the motion before the assembly.

Seventh, *lay on the table*. By the passing of this motion, the immediately pending motion on the floor is set aside. One member moves, another seconds, the chair announces the motion and if there is an immediate majority vote, the motion is adopted. If tabled, the motion may be brought before the assembly again after substantial business of the assembly has transpired. Tabling delays; it does not kill.

The seven subsidiary motions above have only been briefly described. Each motion will be explained in depth in the pages following.

Postpone Indefinitely

"Postpone Indefinitely is a motion that the assembly declines to take a position on the main question." (Robert, pp 105-108). Its purpose is to avoid a direct vote on a motion before the assembly.

Mr. Marchant impetuously moves to bring charges against the treasurer, saying that some money is missing. He says, "I move the treasurer be fired for mishandling the money."

No one else had expected such an outburst, yet no one was suprised when Marchant's buddy, Heinrich, seconded the motion. The assembly was embarrassed and shocked, not only by the charge, but by the unfairness of it, the treasurer's reports having been consistently correct in yearly audits.

Mrs. Gill stood up, and having been recognized by the chair, said, "I move the motion be postponed indefinitely. Three voices shouted, "Second." (It is not necessary that the seconder of a motion be identified, the secretary simply noting in the minutes that the motion had been properly seconded.)

The chair called for debate. Mr. Marchant, being the maker of the motion, had the right to speak first - and he used his right. He continued with his tirade becoming red-faced and abusive - at which point the president reminded Mr. Marchant that he must not abuse another member and that he must confine his discussion of the motion to reasons that the motion should be supported.

The feelings in the assembly began to rise. Mr. Reynolds, after being recognized by the chair, said, "I call the previous question." With a second, the vote was put to the assembly. First, those in favor of the motion to call the previous question (stop debate and vote) stood. The chair, seeing the call for the question was carried overwhelmingly, still called for the negative vote which consisted of two, Mr. Marchant and Mr. Heinrich.

The chair said, "You have voted to call the question. All those in favor of stopping debate will please rise. The tellers will please count and report their counting to the secretary. Be seated. Those opposed rise. The tellers will please count and report their count to the secretary. The motion is adopted (vote counted). The assembly has voted to stop debate and vote on the motion to postpone indefinitely."

The motion to *postpone indefinitely*, requiring only a majority for passage, passed easily, though the chair was careful to take the negative vote. The chair then said to Mr. Marchant, "Mr. Marchant, you have every right to have your charges against the treasurer considered. However, there is a proper method. According to our bylaws, you must put those changes in writing and send them to me. Upon receipt of them the Executive Board will appoint an investigating committee. Please include with your written charges any pertinent data that will substantiate these serious charges you have made against the treasurer.

"There being no other business . . ." (the president looks around for members who want to speak and seeing none says, "The meeting is adjourned."

Procedure in this case has supplanted a great deal of emotion and obvious unfairness to the treasurer, who had been publicly charged without an opportunity to defend himself. The assembly has been embarrassed. Only Mr. Marchant has been accommodated, and he not to the extent he wished. But the combination of bylaws provisions and the procedure to postpone indefinitely prevented further disruption to the organization and unfairness to the treasurer, and placed the burden on Mr. Marchant to identify in writing what he had charged verbally. Also, the time provided for deliberations by the committee to be appointed by the Executive Board - provided Mr. Marchant reduced his charges to writing would allow tempers to cool and emotions to subside.

The procedures to be followed by the committee appointed by the Executive Board were spelled out in the bylaws of the organization.

The Art of Successful Meetings

Amend

General Robert says, "Business is brought before an assembly by the motion of a member. A motion is a formal proposal by a member in a meeting that the assembly take certain action."

How does a member make a motion?

Mr. Rumpole: (rising) Mr. Chairman.

Chair: The chair recognizes Mr. Rumpole.

Rumpole: Mr. Chairman, I move the annual picnic and square dance this year be held at Coogan's Bluff on July 4th, starting at noon."

Mr. Lancet: (without standing simply shouts out) Second.

Chair: It has been moved and seconded the annual picnic and square dance this year be held at Coogan's Bluff on July 4th, starting at noon. You have heard the motion. Is there any discussion?

Main motions require:

Second

Opportunity to Discuss   <u>SDAMR</u>

Opportunity to Amend

Majority vote

Later, opportunity to Reconsider

When the chair asks for discussion of the motion before the assembly, the chair also asks if any member wants to *amend* the motion, to tailor it specifically for the consideration of the assembly. The member may amend in four ways:

By adding words

By inserting words

By striking out words

By striking out and inserting words

Mrs. LaLiberte: (having been recognized by the chair) I move to add the phrase 'to end at 6 P.M.' to the motion.

Chair: (after hearing a second) Is there any debate? The chair, seeing no one seeking the floor, declares the debate closed. All in favor say "aye." Those opposed say "nay." The "ayes" have it, the amendment is adopted.

Mrs. Shallcross: (having been recognized by the chair) I move to insert the words 'fifteenth' between 'the' and 'annual.'

The proposed amendment is seconded, and discussion followed, after which a vote is taken on the amendment, "fifteenth." If passed, "fifteenth" is inserted between "the" and "annual."

Mr. Gray: (having been recognized by the chair) I move to strike out the words 'square dance' from the motion."

The motion was seconded, announced by the chair, discussed, and defeated.

Captain Waters: (having been recognized by the chair) Mr. Chairman, I move to strike out the word 'noon' and insert the words 'eleven o'clock.'

There is a second, the chair announces the proposed amendment, there is discussion, and the amendment is carried.

Chair: We will have our fifteenth annual picnic and square dance this year to be held at Coogan's Bluff on July 4th, starting at eleven A.M. and ending at 6 P.M.

The amended motion is debated further, and then adopted.

The last proposed amendment, to strike out and insert, is one motion, requiring one vote. Strike out is provided above, as is insert. The motion to strike out and insert is one motion, conveniently combining two ways of amending.

Amending a motion allows the assembly to get precisely what it wants, in an orderly manner. A proposed amendment must be voted on first, all amendments requiring a majority vote. Then the vote is taken on the amended main motion.

Substituting a Main Motion for Another

A motion has been made, seconded, and stated by the chair. During the debate following the stated motion, a motion is made to substitute another motion for the pending motion. Though the substitute motion is termed a primary amendment, functionally it acts as a second main motion. The main motion is "perfected" by amendments, if any, and is then set aside for consideration of the substitute. After the main motion and the proposed substitute have been "perfected," the chair asks the assembly if it wishes to replace the main motion by the proposed substitute. If the assembly adopts the substitute motion, the main motion is supplanted by the substitute motion, and the main motion no longer exists. The substitute motion - now the sole main motion - is subject to debate and amendment by the assembly, and acceptance or rejection by majority vote of the assembly.

Possible Scenario

Chair: The chair recognizes the chairman of the Resolutions Committee.

Chairman of the Committee: Mr. Chairman, the Resolutions committee recommends the adoption of the resolution to fund the Outdoors Ministry with $20,000.

Member Echt: Second

Chair: The chair recognizes Pastor Melanchton.

Pastor Melanchton: I move to substitute the following for the pending motion: To substitute "Mission Outreach" for "Outdoors Ministry."

Chair: The amendment is germane for it deals with the use of a fund to be developed, as does the original motion. Is there any discussion of the pending motion, that is, the motion to fund the Outdoor Ministries? The chair, hearing none, now asks. Is there any discussion of the amendment to substitute "Mission Outreach" for "Outdoor Ministries?" (pause) There being no further debate, the delegates will vote on the amendment. Do the delegates want to replace the pending motion, funding "Outdoor Ministries," with the amendment, funding "Mission Outreach?" If the delegates vote to substitute, Outdoor Ministries will no longer be considered. Only Mission Outreach will be considered. If the delegates reject the amendment, "Mission Outreach," then only "Outdoors Ministry" will be considered. The motion before the delegates will then be the pending motion which motion is debatable, amendable and is adopted - or rejected - by majority vote.

Chair: The chair recognizes the substitute motion is complicated. The chair will explain again any part not understood by any delegate.

Chair: (seeing no delegate asking for further explanation) Is there any further debate? Are you ready for the question? Those delegates who favor substituting "Mission Outreach" for "Outdoor Ministries" please raise the a color-coded card.

Chair: The tellers will count, and report their count to the head table.

The chair announces the vote to substitute: In favor, 27 votes, opposed 73 votes. The chair declares the substitute motion defeated.

Chair: The motion now before the assembly is the pending motion, to fund the Outdoor Ministries. **Is there any discussion?**

Abstentions

Q. What does "to abstain" in parliamentary procedure mean?
A. It means a qualified voter decides not to vote.

Q. Is abstaining good or bad?
A. It can be either. If a member abstains from voting because he has a financial interest in a motion being voted on, he should abstain - and that is good. If his brother-in-law will bid on the new roof for the clubhouse, he should abstain from voting. If a member does not vote because he feels he has insufficient information on which to base his vote, that is also good. However, if he gives up his right to participate in decision-making through cowardice or fear of other people's possible reactions, that is bad.

Q. I've heard that an abstention is a "yes" vote. Is that correct?
A. No. An abstention goes with the prevailing side. If a motion passes, an abstention goes with the positive side. If a motion fails, an abstention goes with the negative side. Actually, an abstention is a non-vote.

Q. Suppose there are more abstentions than there are votes. Is the vote taken legal?
A. Yes. The governing document should have the phrase, "present and voting" to insure a legitimate vote. Should ten people vote yes, nine people vote no, and five people abstain, the motion is adopted.

Q. Should the number of abstentions be recorded in the minutes?
A. No. People who abstain have decided not to participate. Their non-participation should not be given prominence.

Q. Should a candidate for office vote for himself? If he does, isn't that egotistical?
A. If he thinks he is the best candidate he should vote for himself. Not to vote for himself when he is best qualified is false modesty.

Substitute Motion Misused

Member #1: Mr. Chairman. I move that we have our annual July outing at Gordon's Grove on July 7th.

Member #2: Second.

Chairman: It has been moved and seconded that we have our annual July outing at Gordon's Grove on July 7th. Is there any discussion?

Member #3: Mr. Chairman. I move that we substitute a boat trip at Waring's Falls on July 7th.

Member #4: Second.

Chairman: It has been moved and seconded that we take a boat trip at Waring's Falls instead. Is there any discussion? Are you ready to vote? (pause) All in favor say 'aye.' (A dozen voices answer.) All opposed say' no.' (Two voices say no.) The 'ayes' have it. We'll go to Waring's Falls.

Tom: Mr. Chairman.

Chairman: Yes, Tom. What is it?

Tom: What happened to the motion to go to Gordon's Grove? We never discussed it.

Chairman: You voted to take the substitute. Since you took the substitute, there was no point in voting on the main motion too. The substitute took the place of the main motion - according to Robert's Rules.

Murmurs of protest and confusion came from the 100-member club. No one knew what to do, but it was clear that many were angry and dissatisfied, several threatening not to go to Waring's Falls.

Was the chairman wrong? If so, wherein did he err?

The first motion was clear enough. While it can be argued that the motion to substitute can be made immediately because it is a primary amendment, and that the general rule is that a primary motion must be voted upon before the main motion is voted upon, there is an inherent difference in a primary amendment by substitution and other primary amendments.

Robert directs that both the main motion and the primary amendment be discussed, functionally causing the main motion and the primary motion to be main motions both being discussed at the same time.

Robert directs that the main motion be given priority attention, that discussion of it be made available first. The maker of the primary amendment to substitute is given opportunity to lead the discussion of the substitute amendment he made <u>after</u> the assembly has "perfected" the main motion.

The chair in this scenario precluded a vote on the main motion by treating the amendment to substitute as if it were a usual primary amendment (to be voted on first), eliminating the main motion by ruling that a vote for the substitute precluded a vote for the main motion. What the chair should have done was to instruct the assembly in the intricacies of substituting. He should say first, "Is there any discussion on the main motion to go to Gordon's Grove?"

Though unlikely that the group would opt to go to both Gordon's Grove and Waring's Falls, it may decide to alternate or to have both at different dates. It is futile to anticipate what a group might do, but the group has the inherent right to discuss and decide what it wants to do. The chair failed in its primary obligation: To have the members of the assembly know what question was being considered, and to give opportunity for all who want to speak to speak. Simply saying "Is there any discussion?" or "Are you ready for the question?" will not suffice if there is confusion among the members of the assembly.

Robert has made clear that parliamentary procedure must not be used to thwart the will of the assembly - as expressed by majority vote - but to facilitate the determination of that will of the assembly. Stating a procedure does not absolve the chair from the obligation to make clear to the members of the assembly what they are voting on.

Sturgis, Demeter, and Keesey consider substitution, though not as extensively as Robert.

Robert states: "A primary amendment to *substitute* is treated similarly to a motion to *strike out and insert*, the paragraph to be struck out being opened to secondary amendment first, then the paragraph to be inserted, after which the vote is taken on whether to make the substitution."

Sturgis considers substitution in ten lines, terming the proposed substitute a primary amendment, ". . . subject only to an amendment to the substitute amendment."

Demeter echoes Robert: ". . . in the case of a substitute motion, the substitute is merely stated by the Chair when proposed, and it is then automatically left unacted on until the pending main motion is first attended to by its being opened to debate and amendment only, not to a final vote; and after the main motion has been perfected as desired, the substitute motion is *then* also automatically open to debate and amendment, so that it, too, can be perfected before a choice between the two is finally made by the body. When the vote is taken, however, the substitute motion is always voted on first (because it is an amendment), after which the main motion is put to a vote as substituted, or as is, if the substitute is defeated, just as on any regular amendment."

Keesey in his usual succinct fashion, considers substitution as any other amendment. He states: ". . . if the vote on the substitute amendment carries, the original main motion is replaced by it; and the new main motion may be further amended before a vote is taken to approve or reject it."

The role of the chair, as always, is to guide the assembly in its deliberations so that it can arrive at the conclusion it seeks. The chair must help insure that the assembly knows what it is voting on, however long or complicated the procedure to gain that end.

The Secretary Erred According to Hettie

Hettie Hepplewhite was furious - and she was going to do something about those August minutes of her union that said she moved to have a Halloween Party for the union's fall Fun Festival! Actually, she had moved for a Caribbean Caprice, and she wanted the record set straight.

At the October meeting of her union she was steaming, impatiently waiting till she could get the floor. Finally the Chair recognized her.

Hettie: The August meeting minutes say I moved for a Halloween Party. I was the one who suggested the Caribbean Caprice.

Chair: Why didn't you make your objection at the September meeting?

Hettie: My sister was ill, and I could not make that meeting.

Chair: If it was not corrected in September, it's too late to correct it now.

Hettie: But the minutes are wrong. Why should I pay for someone else's mistake?

Chair: Under Robert's Rules you should have made your objection in September. If you saw the mistake why didn't you have your good friend Gertrude correct the minutes for you?

Was the chair right? The chair was wrong on several counts:

1. Robert's Rules clearly provide for correcting what has been misrecorded by the secretary. Hettie should moved to "amend" the error in the minutes, and if 2/3 of the members agree with Hettie, a line is drawn through the error in the minutes, and the correct entry is made in brackets thereafter.

2. Hettie should not be penalized for the secretary's error. The minutes must fairly represent what happened in the meeting, and there must be a mechanism for correcting error.

3. Hettie is not required to find the error within a time frame, in this case of one month. If she found the secretary's error a year after it was made, Hettie still has the right to have the error corrected.

4. The secretary made the error, not Hettie. For the chair to interpret Robert's Rules for her own convenience is unethical. If she was not sure, she should have had "Minutes" looked up in Robert's, and delayed a decision until the matter could be researched.

5. The central point remains: the secretary was wrong and Hettie was misquoted. Telling Hettie that she should have Gertrude bring up the objection at the September meeting is to shift blame, and to expect extraordinary activity on two members part when the fault lay elsewhere. Also, the chair personalized a problem, in fact, took a cheap shot at Hettie by bringing Gertrude into the matter.

6. The chair should look at her position and her attitude. As chair, she should help to run meetings fairly and democratically. She should help correct the error in the minutes directly and head on by providing means for correcting errors quickly and quietly, specifically, to amend something previously adopted.

Admittedly, it is difficult for some chairs to preside impersonally, for they cannot consider themselves to be conduits for expressing the real power, that of the members. With power must come restraint, an axiom most obvious in the role of the chair. The unwary or unsophisticated chair who wants to be warm and friendly demeans the seriousness of the organization by trying to substitute good feelings for good presiding. The chair must show tact and a willingness to explain and to help members express themselves; but the thrust of the chair must be: To accomplish the organization's business as democratically and quickly as fairness will allow.

Frank's Fulminations

Frank: (fuming) The language in this meeting is foul and I want a statement placed in the minutes condemning it.

Chairman: All right, Frank, settle down. I'll put your objection in the minutes.

Was Frank right in asking for the statement? Was the Chair right in promising to include the objection?

The answer: Neither was right.

Frank may not determine that a statement of his be entered in the minutes. Minutes consist primarily of actions taken, not discussion concerning them. The fact that Frank wanted his objection entered in the minutes has no standing.

What could Frank have done? He could appeal the decorum of another member, saying, "Mr. Chairman, I appeal the indecorum of Member X. He is loud and abusive."

If Frank's appeal is seconded, the chair puts the appeal directly to the assembly, saying, "Is Frank's appeal the will of the assembly?" If the assembly votes in the affirmative, the Chair admonishes the errant member. If the assembly votes in the negative, the order of the agenda continues as if the appeal had never been made.

Where did the chair err? The chair, in its efforts to mollify Frank, forgot the authority of the organization lies in the assembly. The chair has no more right than any other member to allow Frank's personal complaint to be entered in the minutes.

Consider the possible situations if Frank's personal complaint were entered in the minutes. Every member would then have the same right, and the minutes could easily become a hodge podge of business transacted by the assembly, and personal gripes of the members. The result would be chaos and very lengthy minutes!

Frank evidently thought that his indignation at another member's indecorum sufficient to set aside orderly parliamentary procedure. The member charged by Frank obviously did not consider his words or actions censorable. When there is the heat of conflict, there must be a dependence on procedures agreed upon in quieter moments, and there must be the discipline of the assembly to set aside personal feelings to return to agreed upon procedure.

And those procedures? Minutes consist of:

1. ". . . all main motions

2. ... the wording of the adopted motion, with parenthetical reference to debate and amendments, if any ...
3. ... disposition of the motion
4. ... secondary motions, such as a ballot vote
5. ... all notices of motions to be offered in the future
6. ... all points of order and appeals, whether sustained or lost, together with the reasons given by the chair for his ruling." (Robert, pp 459-460)

Each item in the minutes must have a separate paragraph.

"Respectfully submitted" is an outmoded term. The minutes should be ended with, "Violet Kuehn, Secretary," as an example.

Minutes should be kept permanently. Beyond their immediate use now or in the future is the historical value of minutes of an organization. In Wisconsin, in the fifties, I found old school board minutes that were loosely contained in temporary folders. Though it was not expected that those minutes would be read by anyone at that time, they were important parts of the deliberations of citizens of the school district in the past. I had them bound.

There is a custodial responsibility of the present to preserve past history for the future. The decision to preserve must be made on the basis of continuation of information of the organization, not on the basis of anticipated use, "no one will ever look at these."

Minutes have legal ramifications also. For example, do the minutes of 1990 show a public announcement was made in a regularly called condo meeting that extensive repairs would have to be made in the condo building, costing each unit of the condo thousands of dollars? Or was this information spread informally? The outcome of a law suit depends on the inclusion of public notice in the minutes of the past.

Jerry X maintains he was not notified by the real estate agent that extensive repairs would be made in the building in within the next two years, and that his unit would be assessed several thousand dollars.

The real estate agent searched condo documents to prove the entry in the minutes was made, that the buyer should have been notified by the seller, that the upcoming repairs were common knowledge, and that the real estate agent was not required to tell the buyer. (This sale took place several years ago, before the condo law that now requires notification to the buyer that a special assessment of his condo unit was passed.)

At the time they are written, minutes seem almost trivial, for certainly most entries in minutes are routine and non-controversial. But the judgment about entry or non-entry in minutes must be predicated on consistent procedures of entering.

There can be additional information added to the minutes, such as the names of the seconders of motions, but the names of seconders are not necessary. However, if there is a long-standing custom in an organization to enter the names of seconders in the minutes, that custom should not be discarded because of a sudden strict interpretation of the parliamentary authority. Also, the entry of the gist of the discussion concerning a motion may provide explanation that may be helpful in the future.

A strict procedure for writing and caring for minutes may seem overly demanding - but there will be a great sigh of relief if the careful writing of minutes of the past prevents a law suit in the present.

Questions and Answers

1. Since it takes only a majority vote to accept minutes why does it take a 2/3 vote to amend them?

These minutes had already been adopted. The motion made is to amend something previously adopted. To overrule the majority vote of a previous vote of the membership requires a greater vote than the adoption of them, thus requiring a 2/3 vote.

2. I have heard that an objection to a vote or a procedure must be made when an error occurs. You're saying the error can be corrected years later.

Yes. There must be recourse to correct error, and one recourse is to amend something previously adopted.

3. "Amend something previously adopted" is a big mouthful. Isn't there some way to simplify it?

Unfortunately, no. All five words in the motion are necessary. At first they may seem confusing, but, once explained, they make a great deal of sense.

An Error and a Myth

Friendly Amendment: This is a term that is used widely but enjoys no status as a parliamentary procedure. What it purports to show is reassurance to the maker (first person) that the amender (second person) supports his motion but wants to modify it in a friendly way, of course. Therefore, the amender says, "Would you take a friendly amendment?"

The first person is asked to buy a pig in a poke: If he says yes, he agrees to something, he knows not what. If he says no, then he baldly refuses a "friendly modification" of his motion, and can be considered negative and uncooperative.

As a matter of fact, once the motion is seconded, and repeated by the Chair, the motion belongs to the assembly, not to the original maker. It makes no sense that the maker of the original motion be asked to approve of a modification to a motion that now belongs to the assembly. The maker of the motion has only the advantage of speaking first in debate of the motion.

While the intention of the friendly amendment is laudatory, its implementation causes confusion because the motion belongs to the assembly. The Chair must firmly rule the request out of order, stating that the member may amend the motion, but must direct his proposed amendment to the Chair. Here is reiteration of the salient point that members do not debate laterally, but must speak only to the chair.

Acclamation: Someone moves that Bernice Harris be elected by "acclamation." What is meant is that the mover is requesting unanimous support for Bernice Harris, without debate, without competition.

None of the four parliamentary authorities consulted even mentions the term "acclamation."

There are complications in the attempted use of "acclamation." First, one person is trying to railroad the assembly into acceptance of his choice, trying to get his candidate elected without examination by the voters, trying to avoid the election process because his candidate is so completely deserving. Second, acclamation rushes through a deliberative procedure, election, with unseemly haste, and with superficial consideration of the election process. Third, there must be opportunity for other candidates to be nominated.

The proper procedure is simple. After recognition by the chair, member Maxwell says, "I nominate Bernice Harris." The Chair says, "Bernice Harris is nominated. Are there any other nominations?" The Chair, seeing none, declares nominations closed. "All those in favor of Bernice Harris say 'aye.' Those opposed say 'nay.' The 'ayes' have it. Bernice Harris is elected."

CHAPTER VII - Committees
Proper Use of Committees

One wag said, "America is run on coffee and committees." Another said, "A camel is a horse put together by a committee." A serious observer of American life, however, Tocqueville, that perceptive 19th Century observer of American life, said, "When the Americans have a problem, they set up a committee - and solve it."

But what kind of committee? How is it formed? Who forms it? Robert discusses two kinds of committees: standing, and special (ad hoc, select). Each has a distinct and discrete function.

The standing committee, its name and function, must be found in the bylaws. Its purpose never changes; that is, it serves a continuing need of the organization. For example, the membership committee serves the organization continually. Membership of the committee changes, but the purpose of the committee does not change.

The special committee can be authorized by the assembly at any regular meeting. The committee is charged to make recommendations to the assembly about a specific matter, say, the annual picnic. Once the committee's recommendations are voted on by assembly, the committee, having served its function, goes out of existence.

Committees Provide Five Major Advantages

1. A *small* number of people can meet more often, deliberate more effectively, and work more rapidly than can an assembly. The committee should be small, five members, for instance, though some parliamentarians hold that four members serve better, the quorum of five and four being the same, three - and that it is easier to get four people together than five.

2. The *informal procedures* of a committee allow the chairrman to participate as a member, to make motions; allow members to speak as often and as long as they wish; and allow unlimited debate. While some hold that motions need not be seconded in committee meetings, the practice is suspect and can lead to a lengthy discussion of a matter supported by only one member.

3. *Fewer distractions* in committee meetings provide greater opportunity for quiet deliberations with an increased probability of better reasoned recommendations to the body that created the committee.

4. *Hearings* can provide testimony from expert witnesses and consultants that can prove valuable in the deliberations of the committee.

5. The *privilege of privacy* provides opportunity for the settling of delicate and embarrassing subject matter without publicity, and other problems that are best resolved privately.

Committees may be set up in four ways

1. *Election by ballot* by the assembly. Since any member is qualified to serve on a committee - unless bylaws prohibit - any member's name may be written on a ballot for membership on a committee then being formed. However, nominating from the floor is generally a more efficient and

effective arrangement, for it allows voting on fewer candidates, *all of whose names have been announced by the chair.*

2. *Nomination from the floor* with a voice (viva voce) election. This method has the advantage of speed of selection, a desirable end if the committee's assignment is not controversial. The names of the nominees are known by the members, and a voice vote may be expeditious and democratic.

3. *Nomination by the chair* becomes a decreasingly democratic method of committee member selection. The assumption is that the chair knows those best qualified and interested in serving on the committee. The chair has the obligation to recognize the axiom concerning membership on standing and special committees: members on standing committees should represent the broad spectrum of unlike opinion in the assembly; members on special committees should represent the narrow spectrum of like opinion.

4. *Appointment by the chair* is least democratic in nature, but not necessarily so in practice. The work of the assembly must be carried out, and if there is no objection by the assembly, appointment by the chair may be most easily accomplished and widely accepted. Insistence on serving on committees is more rare than usual.

Unique features concerning committees

Generally, the first person nominated for the committee - assuming his election - becomes the chairman. However, if the nominations to the committee are made from the floor, the assembly should designate the chairman. Otherwise, the committee elects its own chairman on the basis that if the assembly did not designate a chairman, the committee has the right to elect its own chairman.

The power to appoint a committee includes the power to fill any vacancy that arises in it.

Committee recommendations are considered by the assembly. To accept a committee report is to agree with every word in the report.

"Full power" empowers the committee to take reasonable steps to carry out the charge given to the committee by the authorizing body.

A committee report does not require a second - unless the committee is a committee of one - because the report proves it has been supported in committee.

A "minority report" is generally permitted by the assembly, but it is not obligated to permit it.

The minutes of a committee belong to the committee. As a rule minutes are to be confined to the committee to protect its members. However, by a 2/3 majority, or majority of the memebership, minutes of the executive board must be read.

Main motions, incidental main motions, and debatable appeals may be referred to committee.

Large committee meetings are conducted formally; small committee meetings (12 members or fewer) are conducted informally.

A quorum of a committee is a majority of the members of the committee. The quorum of a five-member committee does not change, even if the membership of the committee drops to three. At three, the quorum of a five-member committee is still three.

Special advantages to a nominating committee

The committee can:

Investigate the suitability of potential candidates for nomination;

Secure assurance from persons placed in nomination that they will serve if elected;

Mesh needs of the organization with a balanced committee membership that represents important points of view within the organization;

Develop a slate that will work harmoniously as a committee.

For a committee to function effectively, it must be charged by the authorizing person or group, and must be required to report by a specific day. At the same time, the charge to the committee must not be so vague as to preclude a report within a reasonable time. For instance, no committee should be charged with developing ethical conduct for an organization and be required to report back within a month. Most fatal for the committee system is to allow the committee to report back "when it is ready." As always, reasonableness bridges the gap between charging the committee too tightly and giving it license to proceed as it wishes.

Motion to "refer to a committee" gives time to investigate

Sturgis (p. 166) lists six reasons for referring to a committee:

1. Greater freedom of discussion is possible.
2. More time is available for each subject.
3. Informal procedure can be used.
4. Better use can be made of experts and consultants.
5. Delicate and troublesome questions may be settled without publicity.
6. Hearings may be held giving members opportunity to express their opinions.

Particularly in large groups, such as conventions, it is necessary to require all resolutions - which are only longer and more formal motions - to go first to a Resolutions Committee in order to expedite the work of the convention. The Resolutions Committee must report out the resolutions handed it to the floor, its role being to clarify and cast grammatically those resolutions that come to it.

More often the subsidiary motion to refer to committee is needed because there is a perceived impasse in the assembly, one principal reason being the assembly's lack of information to vote knowledgeably. Supposing the chair wants to refer the proposal to buy a clubhouse to a committee, she says:

"Without objection, the chair will refer the motion on the purchase of a clubhouse to a committee of five. (Pause for three silently counted seconds.) There being no objections, the chair will appoint a committee of five."

The chair is unwise in appointing this committee because the matter to be investigated by the committee involves money, probably considerable money, and it is unwise to spread the responsibility on the choices of the chair.

Were the matter routine, such as creating a committee to provide refreshments and entertainment for the next meeting, the chair would appoint three experienced and recognized members. But in the matter of a clubhouse, a representative committee, elected by the assembly is advisable.

Four ways to set up such a committee are:

1. Nominations and elections by ballot by the assembly.
2. Nominations and elections by the assembly by voice vote.
3. Nominations by the chair, election by the assembly.
4. Appointment by the chair.

Each of the above represents a decreasing democratic involvement of the assembly, #1 being most democratic, #4 being least democratic. Having many assembly members involved in important assembly decisions is a good rule of thumb. The chair especially must avoid making decisions that can be best made by the assembly.

When protests about important decisions come - and they always come - it is better to have the decision made by the ultimate local power, the assembly. It is a great deal more difficult to blame an assembly than the chair.

A member, seeing the impasse on the floor, after recognition by the chair says: "I move that a committee of five, with power, be elected by this assembly, to make recommendations on the matter of the new clubhouse at the next regular monthly meeting.

The chair then repeats the motion, asks for a second. When seconded the chair says, "The motion has been made and seconded. Is there any debate?" OR The chair points out that debate and amendment must be limited to the motion to *refer*, and not to the motion to purchase a clubhouse. In other words, the assembly decides only if it wants a committee, and what it wants the committee to do. The matter of buying or not buying a clubhouse at this time is the matter a committee must discuss.

Later, the assembly will vote on the *recommendations* of the committee after the committee reports at our next regular meeting. Right now we are deciding if we want a committee to work on this matter, or if we want the assembly to decide this matter now. The chair recognizes Mr. Ample.

Mr. Ample: I don't think we need a new clubhouse What's wrong with the old one?

Chair: The chair rules your discussion out of order, Mr. Ample. The chair does not rule you out of order. What you have brought up is to be discussed by the committee - if the assembly wants a committee.

Chair: The chair recognizes Mrs. Prolix.

Mrs. Prolix: What does that phrase 'with power' mean?

Chair: 'With power' means the committee may take reasonable means to secure information to help it in its deliberations. For instance, it may call in expert witnesses, without having to come back and get permission from the assembly. If there is no objection, the chair appoints Members Augustus, Antony, and Lepidus.

Mrs. Prolix: I want to know who's going to be on this committee?

Chair: If there is no objection, the tellers will distribute blank ballots. You will write the name of the person you want to serve on your ballot. Any member is eligible to serve. You may vote for up to five people. If you vote for more, your ballot will not be counted. You may vote for fewer than five, including yourself if you wish. There being no objections, (pause for three silently counted seconds) the chair asks the tellers to distribute the ballots.

> The ballots have been counted. The vote is as follows:
> Mr. Gaunt - 23 votes
> Mrs. Prolix - 21 votes
> Mr. Jejune - 19 votes
> Mrs. Voluble - 17 votes
> Mr. Verbose -16 votes
> Mr. Wordy - 3 votes

The chair declares Mr. Gaunt, Mrs. Prolix, Mr. Jejune, Mrs. Voluble, and Mr. Verbose elected.

Mr. Wordy: Mr. Chairman, you have been unfair. Why did you have to give the votes the people received? Why did you just not tell us which five were elected?

Chair: The chair is required to give the vote counts, even though the results may be disappointing to some people. The committee is charged to come to the next regular meeting with the recommendations concerning the proposal to build a new clubhouse. After the recommendations are made by the committee, the recommendations are subject to debate, amendment, and vote by this assembly. The chair, having no other business, and seeing no member who wants to be recognized, (Chair waits three seconds, then bangs the gavel). This meeting is adjourned.

Of great importance to the assembly is fair representation on the committee of the different points of view in the organization, a responsible committee that works competently and energetically, and an opportunity to debate and vote on the recommendations of the committee.

Why refer the matter to committee? The rationale for referring to a committee is that a few qualified people, working privately, can accomplish more in resolving a problem by developing recommendations for the assembly than the assembly can accomplish by debating a poorly understood issue followed by a doubtful vote.

Handling Committee Reports

The chairman of the Dinner Dance Committee makes a report to the assembled club members. You are presiding. How do you proceed?

You wait for the chairman to make recommendations. If she does not, ask what the recommendations of the committee are.

The chairman, having made the recommendations of the committee, moves the adoption of the recommendations.

You state the recommendations and ask for debate. Many changes may be made in the recommendations, and as long as the assembly agrees, they must be included in the motion. Remember, vote on the amendments first, then the amended motion.

Now the treasurer makes a report. What do you, as the chair, do? Ask if there are any questions first. Then you say, "If there are no objections to the treasurer's report, the report will be filed for audit." Notice, the report is not voted on because members cannot be sure that it is accurate. Filing the report for audit allows a careful scrutiny of it later. It is the report of the Auditing Committee that is voted on. Be sure that the Auditing Committee is competent, especially if it is composed of club members.

If a committee chairman reports on the national convention she attended, what do you do with it? Do you "receive" it?

A report is never received because you already have it. If it is informational, thank the chairperson. If it should be filed, so order. In any case, thank the chairperson and the committee for its work.

Is it a good idea to adopt a committee report?

By adopting a committee report the club is accepting every word in the report. Generally, the club is not interested in how the committee arrived at its recommendations, but rather what those recommendations are. In the original charge of the club, the committee must be instructed to make recommendations and to present those recommendations to the club at a specified date. It does the club no good for a committee to discuss and deliberate if it does not present recommendations for the club to act upon.

As a club member, may I demand to see the minutes of the committee?

You can demand but you may not see. If all the discussions of the committee members were made known to everyone, prudent people would not serve on committees, or the work of the committee would be so stifled by fear of member reactions to what was said in committee that the committee could not function adequately. The club members have a right to know the committee's recommendations, but not how those recommendations were reached.

Conclusion

A committee, composed of a few people, can accomplish what a large group cannot. The committee can concentrate on a problem and recommend to the controlling body. The committee system may sometimes he cumbersome and slow, but it is the best guarantee for the preservation of the rights of the members of the organization the committee serves.

Discharge a Committee

Surprisingly, two of our usually quoted parliamentary experts ignore the motion, Discharge a Committee: Both Sturgis and Keesey disregard what Robert explores at considerable length and Demeter treats tangentially.

A committee had been formed to get bids and make contracts for a typewriter, a desk, and office supplies for the club's office. Over a period of three months, the committee bought and authorized the payment for office supplies but did not seek bids for the typewriter or the desk. The club members are understandably dissatisfied with the progress of the committee.

According to Demeter (p. 83) and Robert (p. 118), a 2/3 vote of the members at a regular meeting is required to discharge the committee. However, where authorized, the supplies bought by the committee remain bought, and must be paid for. The club may not refuse to pay for supplies legitimately bought under the mandate of the committee because the committee failed to act on the typewriter and desk.

A more usual case for discharging a committee takes place when the club votes to decide the issue previously referred to the committee. For example, participation in the annual spring parade of the town is brought back to the club because an early decision about participation must be made to meet a deadline set by the town parade committee. And it is axiomatic in parliamentary procedure that an assembly may not consider the same issue under consideration by one of its committees.

For reasons not readily apparent, the adopted motion to discharge a committee may not be reconsidered; but the defeated motion to discharge a committee can be reconsidered.

Demeter alludes to eliminating a committee by reconsidering the motion that set it up, if done during the same meeting. (p. 87)

There is no apparent barrier to discharging a poorly functioning committee, or a committee whose charge has been reclaimed by the club, at the time of other committee reports. Any committee chairman can be asked, or required, to make a progress report. If the club is dissatisfied, or wishes to consider the committee charge itself, then the club can, by a 2/3 vote of the club members present and voting, eliminate the committee.

The most important aspect of Discharge a Committee is the vote that eliminates the committee, 2/3. That vote restriction casts the motion to Discharge a Committee into the category of demanding better than a majority vote because it rescinds a previous club action. Rescinding previous club decisions requires a 2/3 vote, unless previous notice has been given that a motion to rescind will be made at the next regular meeting. With previous notice, the required vote is a simple majority.

Nominating Committee

To nominate is to name. In parliamentary procedures for non-legislative organizations, to nominate is to put a person's name into consideration, frequently by a nominating committee, for the approval of the parent body that set up the nominating committee. There are advantages to the use of a nominating committee. Members serving on the nominating committee have been selected or elected by an authoritative body. The nominating committee may be (1) selected by the executive board of an organization, if authorized by the bylaws; or (2) be elected by the assembly, either on a voice vote or ballot. The ballot is more democratic because it allows the selection of the nominating committee secretly.

Advantages

A nominating committee can study the needs of an organization and select candidates to satisfy those needs. In this, the first screening process, members are weighed and judged. The committee can interview prospective candidates, can investigate their experience, their qualifications and abilities, and can persuade them to run, or eliminate them as unsuitable.

The nominating committee must secure the consent of its prospective candidates for office to agree to run, and to serve if elected. The assumption that all persons who run must necessarily want to be elected in order to serve is erroneous. Human nature being unpredictable, the nominating committee must have a clear and unequivocal agreement of all the candidates that they will run if nominated, and serve if elected.

That agreement may not be given only to a single member of the nominating committee during a happy hour some Thursday afternoon. While the candidates may not reasonably be expected to make declarations in writing, they must make known their intentions to at least two committee members. It is recognized that the formality proposed above is generally unnecessary, but the parliamentarian must deal with defensible procedures, not hoped for probabilities.

The nominating committee is able to apportion representation equitably among different groups and different areas. Ed Winter may be put on the nominating committee because of his continuing focus on retirement benefits, representing the interests of a bloc of the members. Michelle Rogers may be put on the committee because she represents the interests of the under-35 age group.

Of course the selection process is not as mechanical as the above would indicate, nor do people have only one interest. Other factors of intelligence, stability, and industry must be kept in mind, including the specialized areas of interests of the members of the organization. Area-wise representation must reflect the different geographical regions served by the organization. One dramatic example of regional representation in the political area is the necessary appointment of school board members in New York City. If a city-wide election were held, Brooklyn, the most heavily populated borough, could elect all the school board members, effectively disenfranchising the other four boroughs. The school board members thus elected would have little direct concern about school matters important to the other four boroughs.

The nominating committee serves as the first selection barrier to be passed by the candidates. The nominating committee, knowing the membership, selects the best candidates they can agree upon, dismissing those whose popularity may be greater than their abilities. The committee serves as an assembly in miniature, selecting, discarding, agreeing on members to be finally considered by the parent assembly.

Composition

The committee needs to represent different points of view. Michael Seger wants the organization to become larger by loosening what he considers stringent requirements for membership. Tony Keating wants to keep the organization small with a clear focus on the aims and functions of the organization. Both points of view can be represented on the nominating committee. Such representation cannot be allowed to press a narrow agenda that precludes compromise on the candidates selected by the committee, that is, each individual insisting on having his own selection. Though sometimes painful, non-unanimous committee votes will be necessary to resolve the differences. All committee members must expect to win sometimes and lose sometimes, to be modest when they win, and gracious when they lose.

Former officers of the organization can be good nominating committee members because they have worked intimately with the needs of the organization and the members of it. It would be profligate to ignore the dozens of years of experience of past officers for their experiences are unique and valuable.

A nominating committee of ten to fifteen members is unusual, depending on the size of the organization. Many small non-profit organizations are fortunate to have three people to serve. Potential officers should not be placed on the nominating committee to prevent their serving as officers. It is legal for members of the nominating committee to nominate their own members, but it is not expedient. There is an air of favoritism sensed by the members if the nominating committee names one of its own members because there is the appearance of giving that person an unfair advantage over other members.

A balance to the committee is desirable, but that balance must not be achieved by trade-offs that hurt the work of the committee. Having minority, gender, and race, and age representation on a committee is desirable; but the main purpose of the committee is to name the best people for officership. If by having various segments of the organization represented there is a quota element that allows one person to be selected simply because he is young can adversely affect the effectiveness of the committee. On one government committee a representative committee was set up to write bylaws for the group. The only trouble was no one on the committee could write bylaws, and the one person knowledgeable in the field was excluded because there was already a person of his age, gender, and racial makeup on the committee.

Formation

The process for nominating and electing members to leadership roles should be spelled out in the bylaws. Certainly careful preparation should be made to set up a committee that will serve the needs of the organization. The most democratic way to name members for a nominating committee is to have them elected by members of the assembly. The names can be shouted out, or they can be written confidentially. The latter is the more democratic.

Sometimes the executive board, especially if it is large enough, can appoint the nominating committee. However, here again the possibility of favoritism or cronyism adumbrates this method. Having the executive board, composed of the officers of the organization, appoint a nominating committee removes the nominating process so far from the members of the assembly that it is universally suspect. Having the president name the nominating committee members is flat out forbidden in properly run organizations.

Function of the nominating committee

1. To select the best candidates for the open positions on the board;

2. To meet and discuss personalities, needs of the organization, and the means to mesh the two;

3. To secure permission of those selected to run, and their promise to serve if elected;

4. To report the committee's findings at the appropriate time;

5. To accept the possibility that nominations from the floor may negate what the committee has done;

6. To remain a committee until officers have been elected and have taken office; to stand to provide additional candidate(s) if an office is not filled.

One continuing problem in the process of nominations from the floor is the frequent bylaws provision that biographical data for each candidate must be provided the members of the assembly before that person may be considered for office. The problem happens frequently in multiple-day conventions. One solution is to set a deadline for submission of biographical data for those nominated from the floor. It is grossly unfair to have candidates with biographical data and candidates without biographical data running in the same race.

Many large organizations have found including each candidate's photograph with biographical data helpful.

Report of Committee

The chairman of the nominating committee usually presents a written slate to the secretary after he has read the recommendations of the nominating committee.

Chairman: Mr. President, the nominating committee presents the following slate. (Chairman reads the slate.)

President: Thank you, Mr. Chairman. Are there additional nominations for president? There being none (pause), the Chair declares the nominations for president closed.

The same procedure is used for each office.

Supposing the nominating committee proposes one person for each office, the argument can be made that a vote is unnecessary, that the whole slate be adopted. But if it is, and you want to nominate a person for the secretary's job, you are inhibited, if not prohibited, from doing so. The greater danger is the acceptance of the nominating slate as the assembly's slate, without proper participation of the assembly. In effect, the nominating committee becomes the assembly, and nominations by the nominating committee insure election to office.

If the Chair offers the opportunity for nomination from the floor only for the whole slate, a member may hesitate to nominate another person for the secretary's position, for example, because of the confusion that might ensue when the election of the president has not been completed.

The list of candidates for each office - plus nominations from the floor - are read out by the chairman of the nominating committee. Thereafter, the Chair announces after the election of each officer, "The Chair declares Member_____ to be vice president (or secretary or treasurer)."

The nominating committee is automatically discharged upon the election of the new officers. However, should one newly elected officer refuse, or be unable to serve, the nominating committee must meet again to propose a candidate for the open position.

It is recommended that new officers be elected near the end of the meeting by the then current officers. While other business of the assembly is being considered, the tellers may retire to tabulate the votes, and then report back to the assembly. An alternative in a small organization is a recess of the assembly while the votes are being counted.

Alice Sturgis describes the nominating committee, saying, "The nominating committee is one of the most important committees of an organization because it can help to secure the best officers" (p.149), thus promoting the future health and vigor of the organization.

Questions and Answers

1. Why must nominations and elections be so formal? Why can't people just agree among themselves without all the meetings and reporting?
Probably many organizations follow the informal procedure you ask about. There is no need for rainwear when the sun is shining. However, it is better to use formal procedures that vex people than to use informal procedures that confuse and anger people.

2. Why do you recommend ballots instead of raising hands? It is a lot faster to use hands than to write out and count ballots.
What you say is true, hand-raising is faster than balloting; but speed in procedures can produce haste, and haste can cause confusion, and confusion anger. By proper balloting the vote of the individual member is confidential, the results are written and can be verified, and the final results cannot be validly questioned.

The Committee of the Whole, The Quasi-Committee of the Whole and Consider Informally

Keesey (p. 84) lambasts the concept of the Committee of the Whole, writing, "The artificiality of a group referring the consideration of a motion to itself, under the pretense that functioning as a single large committee will allow it to proceed more effectively in its deliberations, approaches the ridiculous. And when the group later moves to Rise and Report to itself, in order to shed its playacting roles as a committee and resume normal status, the ludicrousness of the situation is undeniable. Perhaps that is why these motions are never used in most organizations."

Demeter (p. 285) supports the procedure, providing the modern form. ". . . that we go into a committee of the whole," for four reasons:

1. because the question is compelling or unusual;

2. a decision must be made quickly while the assembly is still in session;

3. there is no time for a committee to be formed and to function;

4. to afford the members greater freedom in debate, thus permitting greater clarification of the question.

Sturgis (p. 185) dismisses the Committee of the Whole by pointing out the abandonment of the motion by most organizations, and recommending the use of Informal Consideration.

Robert (pp 521 - 535) details at exhaustive length the forming of the Committee of the Whole and the limitations that must be observed while the assembly is so constituted. His encyclopedic descriptions exhaust any but the most ardent addicts of parliamentary procedure. He details what other parliamentary authorities accept as "givens," that a person may raise a parliamentary inquiry in a Committee of the Whole, for instance.

One distinguishing feature of the chair in Committee of the Whole is the replacement of the presider with another person, because of possible conflict of interest for the presider, or because the presider wishes to debate the question as a member of the organization. The replacement of the presider with a non-controversial person is central to the democratic atmosphere of fair and full inquiry. The secretary may serve, or anyone else chosen by the chair. The temporary presider holds the gavel until after the resolution of the pending question, and then returns the gavel to the authorized presider.

Quasi-Committee of the Whole

Demeter (p. 289) gives a brief description of Quasi-Committee of the Whole, dismissing it by recommending Committee of the Whole, or Informal Consideration.

Sturgis ignores Quasi-Committee of the Whole. Keesey also ignores Quasi-Committee of the Whole.

Robert (pp 522-532) touches briefly on Quasi-Committee of the Whole.

The only difference between Committee of the Whole and Quasi-Committee of the Whole is that the Chairman steps aside in Committee of the Whole, and the Chairman remains the chair in Quasi-Committee of the Whole.

It may be that a quarrelsome motion before the assembly, one that does not represent a conflict of interest for the chair, can best be treated by Quasi-Committee of the Whole. The Chair may ask for unanimous consent, saying, "The issue requires consideration that can best be provided by resolving the assembly into a Quasi-Committee of the Whole. If there are no objections, the assembly will be resolved into a Quasi-Committee of the Whole. The Chair, seeing no objections, declares the assembly resolved into a Quasi-Committee of the Whole."

After the Committee of the Whole has completed its deliberations, the chair declares, "Without objection, the Quasi-Committee of the Whole is resolved into the assembly."

Consider Informally

At a time when organizations' rules are becoming more sophisticated, and board meetings are open meetings, the use of "consider informally" begins to take on an increasing importance. The motion is a variation of refer to a committee. Its principal result is the elimination of the limitation on the number of times a member may speak. Its particular value to the organization is to allow an authoritative board to function like a committee, though the people involved are the same.

Consider informally is an incidental motion, meaning, it is incidental to the motion being considered. The assembly, decides that its deliberations on a motion can be more effective if there is no immediate possibility of a vote being taken on them. Considering informally removes that possibility, for while considering informally, the assembly may not take a final vote on the motion being considered informally.

The informality of the committee's activities applies only to the removal of the limit on speeches. Formal minutes are kept and retained; other motions can be made under regular rules of order.

At first blush, it appears consider informally is another parliamentary procedure that is archaic and useless. It is true that the motion is rarely used, but it has value for members can be more free in informal discussions without the weight of a vote pending.

Once the main motion is ready for vote of the assembly, a motion is made that ". . . the regular rules of debate be in force," or that ". . . the question be considered formally."

Upon a majority vote, the assembly reconstitutes itself completely, adopts or rejects the motion considered informally, and then goes on to other items of business. (Robert, pp 533 - 4)

Demeter (pp 284-5) corroborates Robert's views on informal consideration. He does stress the importance of maintaining procedural discipline while the assembly considers a matter informal, adding the cogent thought, " . . . there is no easier or surer way to deliberate upon and to transact a piece of business than by observance of the rules and proprieties of parliamentary etiquette."

Sturgis (pp. 128-9) adds, "Sometimes an assembly wishes to consider a problem that is not sufficiently understood . . . There may not be time to refer the problem to a committee . . . Rather than offer a poorly thought-out motion, which will consume time and effort to perfect by amendment, it is better to consider the problem informally and then formulate a good motion."

Both Demeter and Robert indicate that the use of Informal Consideration is preferable to the clumsy - and in Keesey's thinking "ridiculous" procedures of Committee of the Whole and Quasi-Committee of the Whole. Even Keesey has a tangential support for Informal Consideration, though he feels a recess may serve the assembly's need better. (p. 85)

CHAPTER VIII - More Subsidiary Motions
Scenario for "postpone to a certain time"

"It is improper . . . to postpone anything beyond the next session which would be an attempt to prevent the next session from considering the question." (Robert, p. 54)

It is proper to postpone a matter to the next meeting for a number of reasons such as allowing tempers to cool, allowing more time to accumulate pertinent data, or to prevent a decision based on inadequate data. Consider the following scenario.

Chair: The chair recognizes Mr. Able.

Mr. Able: Mr. Chairman, we have been arguing about the cost of renovations for the clubhouse for the last twenty-eight minutes. I move that the chair appoint a committee of three people to make recommendations to this assembly.

Chair: Is there a second?

Mr. Baker: I second.

Chair: It has been moved and seconded that the matter of renovations to the clubhouse be referred to a committee of three set up by the chair.

Mr. David: I move that the matter of clubhouse renovations be postponed to the next meeting.

Mrs. Edward: Second.

Mr. Abel: You can't do that. You are putting two motions before the assembly at the same time. My motion comes first.

Chair: The motion is in order. In the precedence of motions, the motion to postpone to a certain time outranks the motion to set up a committee. The motion to postpone to the next meeting must be acted on next by this assembly.

Mr. Hardy: Why not postpone the motion to the July meeting. By that time our CD will come due and we'll have more money.

Chair: The club may have more money, but the June meeting may not be skipped. Members must have a right to decide about the renovations. Please understand. If the assembly votes to postpone to the next meeting it simply means that the next regular meeting assembly will adopt or defeat the motion.

Mrs. Loll: I move adjournment.

Mr. Mumm: Second.

Chair: The motion to adjourn has been moved and seconded. Since the motion is in connection with a motion already before the assembly, there is no debate or amending, just a majority vote to adjourn or not to adjourn.

Mr. Abel: What is all this trickery? I want a committee to work on the renovations, and before my motion is voted on, there is a motion to postpone to the next meeting, and now this motion to adjourn. I think we should vote on my motion first.

Chair: The motion to adjourn is indeed in order. If the assembly wants to adjourn before deciding anything more, it is clearly authorized to do so. Once again, the precedence of motions permits adjournment under these circumstances. All in favor say "aye." Those opposed say "nay." The chair is in doubt. Will the tellers prepare to count? All those in favor, rise. Please be seated. All those opposed, rise. Please be seated. The chair rules the motion to adjourn is defeated. (It is generally better to take a standing counted vote, unless the vote clearly shows the adoption or defeat of the motion.)

The motion now before the assembly is to postpone definitely to the next meeting. If the assembly so votes, the secretary will place the item on the agenda of the next regular meeting. Is there further discussion of the motion to postpone the consideration of the clubhouse renovations to the next meeting? The chair, seeing none, calls for all those in favor of the motion to vote "aye." Those opposed vote "no." The chair rules that the motion is adopted, and this matter will be an item on the agenda of the next regular meeting.

Ms. Secretary, will you please see to it that the item on clubhouse renovations is placed on the agenda of the next regular meeting. (Raps the gavel.)

The next item of business is . . .

While there is much repetition in the above scenario, repetition is necessary for clarity, and to reduce potential confusion. It is better to repeat even when repetition appears unnecessary than to be charged with railroading by someone opposed to the adopted motion.

In chairing, one avoids shortening the meeting by acting on the basis that everyone knows what the motion on the floor is. Many may have forgotten or become confused about the matter before the assembly. Of course, members have a right - and a duty - to keep informed.

Anytime a member is not sure of the motion on the floor, or the procedure required, that member has a right to make a parliamentary inquiry or raise a point of order. The member can be sure that what he is asking about is likely confusing a number of other people. But even if the member is alone in his confusion, he has a right to understand what he is being asked to vote on.

Sometimes one hears a motion to "table until the next meeting." This motion is incorrect because to "table" or to "lay on the table" is restricted to the current session or meeting. To postpone to the next regular meeting requires an adopted motion to postpone to a certain time, or to postpone definitely.

Motion to limit debate is not a debatable motion

Three principal complaints about meetings are: they last too long, they're boring, and some members talk too much. A carefully designed agenda and a crisp pace will largely eliminate the first complaint. Meetings are boring because members are not involved, either through lack of interest or knowledge of what to do to promote their own interest. Additionally there are easy and available means to keep people from talking too much, exemplified in the procedure to limit or extend debate.

At the beginning of the meeting, the chair can propose that each agenda item be limited to twenty minutes, and each speaker limited to two minutes each time he or she speaks. The chair says, "If there are no objections, each agenda item will be limited to twenty minutes, and each member limited to two minutes each time that member speaks. Should the assembly want to extend time for discussion, it can do so with a 2/3 vote on a motion made and seconded." The proposed motion will probably carry for two reason: the limitations to limit the time for an agenda item and the time for an individual member appear reasonable; and it is difficult to foresee a motion that will require more than the allotted time. Robert (p. 162 *passim*) states the motion to limit or extend debate can be applied to any debatable motion.

The motion to limit debate is not debatable, but it can be amended. For example, Mr. George moves that the meeting run no later than 11 P.M. The motion is seconded and put before the assembly for vote. Mr. Lake moves to amend the motion, calling for the meeting to end no later than 10:30 P.M. No one may debate either Mr. Lake's motion nor Mr. George's amendment. The chair then asks for the vote on the 10:30 P.M. limitation first. If accepted the limitation is be set at 10:30 P.M.

It can be argued by the pedants that since only the amendment has been adopted, the main motion with the adopted amendment must be voted on. But the amendment functions as a substitute motion in this case, and it is picayunish to waste time with a slavish obedience to form that changes nothing.

To limit or extend debate requires a 2/3 vote for adoption because of the fundamental rule that any procedure that limits the right of the assembly to debate requires a 2/3 vote. Even extending the time for debate limits the assembly because it sets a limit.

A basic rule in parliamentary procedure holds that a defeated motion may not be renewed again at the same meeting, unless it is changed substantially. Interestingly, the motion to limit or extend debate may be renewed unchanged if substantial change has been made in the motion to which it is attached. The motion to limit or extend debate is not changed; the motion to which it is attached is changed. Usually, the motion to limit or extend debate applies to the pending motion, though it can be specified to include other motions. For instance, if a main motion has been amended, the motion to limit debate applies only to the amendment, though it may apply to the main motion if so moved. A decision by the assembly extending debate affects only the motion to which it attached, not any subsequent motion.

There are two obvious reasons that a member moves to limit debate: stopping the assembly from full debate, and forcing a resolution after enough debate. The former rarely happens for it requires an unusual determination predicated on self interest and skill in parliamentary procedure. The second usually finds the necessary 2/3 easily, for it is probably true that the member moving to limit debate voices the desire of many other people.

The form of the procedure is simple:

Chair: The chair recognizes Mr. Mainwaring

Mr. Mainwaring: I move to limit debate to ten more minutes.

Several voices: Second.

Chair: Are you ready for the question.? (3 second pause). Since this motion requires a 2/3 vote, the chair asks the tellers to stand by. All in favor, please rise. (Tellers count, and bring their tallies to the secretary.) Please be seated. All opposed, please rise.

(Tellers count, and bring their tallies to the secretary. The secretary totals the numbers given for both positive and negative, and gives the total to the Chair.)

Chair: There are sixty votes in favor, thirty votes opposed. The motion is carried. Debate is limited to ten minutes more, and will stop no later than 10:08 P.M.

An easy way to compute 2/3 vote is to double the negative vote. If it does not *exceed* the positive vote, the motion is adopted. Voting by raising hands is more accurate than a voice vote; voting by standing vote is more accurate than a vote by raising hands; voting by standing counted vote is most accurate of all.

"Lay on the Table" Superior to "Previous Question"

The wrangle about raising dues had been raging for thirty minutes and the members were getting restless. Suddenly, Jack Rogers shouted out "Question. Call the question." Bob Boyles who was presiding said, "The question has been called for. All those in favor say 'aye.' Those opposed say 'no.' There is a clear majority. The question is adopted." What did Boyles do wrong ? A better question would be, what did he do *right*?

Calling for the question - which means stop debating and vote - requires 2/3 vote because it limits the assembly's right to deliberate. Any motion that limits the assembly's right to deliberate - limit or extend debate, close nominations, expel from membership, amend the constitution, and suspend the rules are prominent examples - requires a 2/3 vote. In voting, there are the extremes of unanimous vote or no votes. Most votes are majority, that is, at least one more member votes for a motion than votes against it. However, in very serious matters, as those listed above, there is a need for more than a majority, and less than a unanimous vote, and the usual answer is 2/3. One organization that required a 98% vote to change the constitution, an anomaly that probably represents past difficulties in voting that were offset by the unwise requirement that 98% of the members agree on any matter.

When the chairman hears "Question" shouted out, he should ignore the shout for the following reasons: In order to call the question, the person making that motion must be recognized by the chair. When recognized by the chair, the member says, "Mr. Chairman, I call for the question." His motion must be seconded. There is no debate, and an immediate vote must be taken; 2/3 in the positive stops debate and requires a vote on the pending motion.

In cases of motions that arouse strong feelings in the members, the chair needs to take a conservative voting approach. For instance, taking a voice vote is suspect because what the chairman considers a clear vote for closing debate and voting, members opposing may later claim was not a clear vote. Never mind that the negative voters are wrong, they can still grumble. Even worse is calling for a raising of hands because of the inherent difficulties connected with that form of voting, especially in a group larger than thirty people. With advance planning members could raise colored cards or in the case of one annual convention of some 700 delegates, the members raise their frisbees.

An effective step for the chair, or a member, is to ask for a standing vote. If those voting for the motion to close debate and vote are in overwhelming numbers, the chair can then say, "It is obvious that more than 2/3 have voted for the motion to stop debating and vote. We will now vote on the motion before you."

Still there is recourse for the negative voters. A member can say, "I appeal the decision of the chair," or "I doubt the vote." The chair then should ask for unanimous consent to appoint tellers, and have a standing counted vote. Any member may demand a standing vote, but only the assembly can authorize a standing counted vote. What the chair must keep in mind is that the vote to stop debate and vote is just that - it does not affect the motion on the floor. So, after the assembly votes to stop debate and vote, the chair calls for the vote on the motion on the floor which usually takes a majority vote. Assuming the motion to stop debate and vote passes, two possibilities exist for the vote on the motion on the floor: If the motion passes, the chair goes to the next item; if the motion fails, it may not be considered again in the meeting. Assuming the motion to stop debate and vote is defeated, debate continues on the motion on the floor as if the motion to stop debate and vote had not been made.

The motion to stop debate and vote can be made at any time unless the chair perceives the motion to be dilatory or obstructive. In that case, the chair says, "Because the motion to stop debate and vote has been defeated once, the chair rules the motion dilatory at this time, and disallows it." Immediately the maker of the motion appeals the decision of the chair. Since the assembly has just defeated the motion to stop debate and vote, it seems most likely that the assembly will support the decision of the chair, and continue to debate the motion on the floor.

While the above seems elaborate - and in many cases it is - the chair must nevertheless preside conservatively, presiding in such wise that future complaints can be offset by proven procedure that protects both the affirmative and the negative voters. Specifically, when the vote on a controversial issue has been resolved by a standing counted vote by tellers and the results are reviewed by the secretary and one other person, there can be no legitimate complaint about the voting, unless the person so complaining can prove that the chair, the tellers, the secretary and the other person, were all colluding to defeat the will of the assembly, almost an impossibility.

If a series of amendments to the bylaws are being debated, a member may move to stop debate and vote ('the previous question motion") on one, some, or all of the pending amendments. For example, if the member calls the question on amendments #1, #3, and #5, and the motion is seconded, amendments #2, and #4 are untouched. The motion to select the amendments to be voted on can be predicated on the member's judgment that #1, #3, and #5 will pass easily, that #2, and #4 will require more debate.

If the member calls the question, that means he is asking for a vote on the last amendment only. If the member calls for "all pending motions," that means he is asking for all five amendments. After the amendments have been thoroughly debated and there is general support for each of the amendments, calling the question on all pending motion can save time, and still reflect the judgment of the members.

There is an additional safeguard built into the motion to "call the previous question." The adopted motion can be reconsidered by majority vote. Robert (p. 23 t) says the vote can be reconsidered ". . . only before any vote has been taken under it." In other words, once action flowing from the vote on the motion on the floor has been taken, reconsideration may not be considered. Keesey (p. 86) discusses his substitution for 'the previous question' by calling the term so artificial it needs translating, advocating the term "Close Debate." He uses one paragraph of ten lines whereas Robert uses twelve pages! Sturgis (pp 69, 70) takes a page to describe what she calls "The motion to vote immediately." While she offers more detail than Keesey, she avoids the lengthy explanations of Robert. Demeter (pp 93-98) takes the most conservative position of the four major parliamentary authority, stating (p. 93, ". . . the correct form is to 'move the previous question," instead of 'I move that discussion and amendments cease." Demeter differentiates between calling the question and moving all amendments and cease debate. A member could move to stop all amendments and vote, or stop all debate and vote. Either one requires a 2/3 vote, and seems hair splitting. If there can be no amendments, there can still be debate of the motion before the house. If there can be no further debate, the only logical next step is to vote.

Calling for the previous question (stop debating and vote), requires satisfaction of the following requirements:
1. May not interrupt when another has the floor
2. Must be seconded
3. May not be debated
4. May not be amended
5. Requires a 2/3 vote
6. Only the affirmative may be reconsidered

Since "lay on the table" ranks superior to the "previous question," the previous question may be laid on the table and not carried into effect immediately. However, if the motion for the previous question is laid on the table, it may be taken from the table by that motion after "substantial business" has transpired after the motion has been laid on the table.

Ira Harris' Distress

Ira Harris was nervous and anxious. This was his first meeting as president. What he really wanted was to get the meeting over, and go to Florida. But before he could leave, he had to finish the meeting - and get past Rob Cobb. Rob had been quiet up to now, but Ira knew he was just waiting for a chance to disrupt the meeting. Finally Rob got his chance.

Discussion of a dues increase had been droning on for forty minutes. The members of the county-wide Realtors' association were getting restive - and Ira's ulcer was beginning to act up.

While Sally Smart was attacking the motion at microphone three, Rob shouted, "Question, question. Let's have the #*@#*! question."

Ira: (turning desperately to his experienced parliamentarian whispering) What'll I do?

Quentin Quick: Ignore him. He's out of order.

Ira: Here, you take over. (Then, turning to the 200 Realtors assembled in their monthly meeting) The parliamentarian will explain what to do."

Quentin Quick: As parliamentarian to the chair, ordinarily I do not speak directly to the assembly. However, the chair has asked me to speak. And if there is no objection, I'll answer the question. A member may not just call out "question" and thereby stop the deliberations of the Realtors, and force a vote. In fact, even a majority of the members may not stop the debating and vote, which is what "Calling the Question" really is. Further, for anyone to call the question, that person must have the floor - and the person shouting out "Question, question" certainly did not have the floor.

Chair: The motion before the assembly is the raising of dues. Is there further discussion? The chair recognizes Ray Raxstraw.

Ray Raxstraw: Mr. Chairman, I call for the question.

Several Voices: Second.

Chair: It has been moved and seconded that the assembly stop debating and vote. This motion is undebatable and is not amendable. The assembly will vote at this time. Calling the question requires a 2/3 vote, which means we must have a <u>standing</u> vote. If there is no objection, the chair calls for a standing, <u>counted</u> vote.

Tellers, please take your positions. You will work in teams, as previously set up. Both tellers will count their assigned areas, and will report their matching votes to the secretary. If the separate counts do not match, the tellers will recount.

The chair reminds the assembly that only the motion to stop debating and voting is being voted on. The vote on raising dues will follow if this motion is adopted. All members in favor of stopping the debate and voting, please rise. The tellers will count. Please be seated. All those opposed, please rise. The tellers will count. Please be seated.

The secretary reports there are 62 votes in favor, 16 votes opposed. The motion to call the question is adopted.

Dora Dull: Are you trying to pull a fast one? You didn't compare the ayes and the nays. Nobody could figure that fast. You have to add up the positive and the negative votes, then take 2/3 of the total. There's no other way."

Chair: The chair points out there is another way. By doubling the negative vote, we get the same result, but much faster. If the doubled negative vote is not <u>greater</u> than the positive vote, then the motion passes by 2/3. Since the negative vote of 16 doubled is no <u>greater</u> than the positive vote of 32, the motion passes by 2/3 vote.

You have decided to vote on the raise in dues. The dues motion is a main motion and requires only a majority vote. All in favor, please rise. The tellers will count. Be seated. All those opposed, please rise. The tellers will count. Be seated. The motion to raise dues $10 per month is adopted by a vote of 60 to 18.

Chair: (raps the gavel then says immediately) The next item of business is selecting the site of our annual convention.

It is axiomatic in parliamentary procedure that the presider takes extra care, even extraordinary care, when the matter before the assembly is controversial. Above, while a standing <u>counted</u> vote for the dues motion is not <u>required</u>, its use is prudent, for the actual vote will be recorded in the minutes, and will preclude any future substantial objection to the chair's handling of this controversial issue.

Briefly, limiting the right of the assembly to debate requires a 2/3 vote. Other examples of motions requiring a 2/3 vote are: Calling the question, Limiting or Extending Debate, and Closing Nominations. The competent presider avoids actions that can be described by opponents as railroading. Whenever the chair is in doubt, it should have as standing counted vote by <u>tellers</u>, not by the chair or people at the head table. While having people rise and sit, then rise and sit again may appear unreasonable or unnecessary, it is better to be considered too conservative than to be charged with inadequate presiding. It is far better to take a standing counted vote when not sure than to assume that people will agree with the chair's evaluation of a vote, especially when the vote is close and the issue controversial.

One final note on Call the Previous Question. It is proper, though unusual, for a member to move to Lay on the Table the call for the previous question. Opponents to the Previous Question motion may gain some time because Lay on the Table requires only a majority vote. However, in non-legislative assemblies Lay on the Table does not kill a motion, it postpones it only to later in the same meeting or to the following regular meeting.

Lay on the Table

When Demeter discusses Lay on the Table, the seventh and highest ranked of the seven subsidiary motions, he points out an interesting rationale for ranking subsidiary motions. "... It was decided to base their rank on the speed and wisdom with which each motion can accomplish business." In short, the faster the subsidiary motion can resolve the pending motion, the higher it is in the precedence of motions.

Since Lay on the Table sets aside the pending question only temporarily, it is easier to bring back and resolve the pending question. Lay on the Table is not a motion to kill a motion - Postpone Indefinitely can do that - but simply sets a motion aside until other substantial business is completed. Later, in the same meeting, or in the following regular meeting, Lay on the Table may be brought back before the assembly by the mirror-image motion, Take from the Table. Once a motion to Lay on the Table is made, seconded, and announced by the chair, it requires only a simple majority to delay consideration of the pending question. Delay is emphasized for in some legislative assemblies, to Lay on the Table is to kill a motion or resolution. In non-legislative assemblies, Lay on the Table simply delays assembly action.

Lay on the Table, while simple in execution, is controversial in nature. Some parliamentary authorities refuse to recognize the motion. Keesey lists Lay on the Table in his chapter on "Motions Not Recommended," saying: "Two good reasons for dropping this motion are that it does not mean what it says, and that its intended use has been generally abused. The consideration of a motion is never literally laid on the table, or tabled . . . The purpose of this motion - to put aside temporarily the consideration of a motion - is well served by the motions to Postpone or to Recess. . . . If one's intent is to kill the motion, the motion To Withdraw should be used." Alice Sturgis also opposes the term "Lay on the Table" preferring Postpone Temporarily. "'To Lay on the Table' grew out of the legislative custom of laying a bill on the clerk's desk awaiting further consideration . . . the term 'postpone temporarily' is clear and satisfactory."

The parliamentary maze above is easily solved: Follow the parliamentary authority stipulated in the constitution or bylaws of your organization. If your organization uses Robert's Rules - and reportedly 90% of organizations use Robert's Rules - simply follow the instructions of Robert:

1. Requires recognition by the chair

2. May not interrupt the person holding the floor

3. May not be debated nor amended

4. Requires a majority vote

5. May not be reconsidered.

Sometimes the phrase "Table to the next meeting" is used. The intention is correct - delay - but the delay cannot be so stipulated, because the tabled motion may be brought before the assembly at the same meeting, after substantial business has been accomplished by the assembly. The motion the chair needs to use is Postpone to a Definite Time, which means the next regular meeting. The motion to Lay on the Table must be considered before the end of the next regular meeting or it expires.

There is some debate among parliamentarians whether the chair should bring the tabled motion before the assembly at the next regular meeting. There are two points of view. One view holds that the chair should not bring the tabled motion to the attention of the assembly because by so doing the chair gives inferential support to the motion. The maker of the motion should be present to take the motion from the table, or should have a like-minded person move to take the motion from the table. The other point of view is the *importance* of the tabled motion determines if the tabled motion is presented to the assembly by the chair. For instance, if a decision on sending delegates to an upcoming convention must be made before the next regular meeting - the convention being scheduled before the next regular meeting - then the chair should bring the matter to the assembly for decision.

Generally, the maker of the motion to Lay on the Table should be responsible for taking the motion from the table. But circumstances, such as the convention problem, require the use of judgment on the part of the chair, not blind obedience to a conviction.

As usual there is a middle ground: the chair can inform both supporters and opponents of the tabled motion that the motion must be considered at the current meeting so that the assembly can decide about sending delegates to the convention. The stress here is informing both sides lest the chair be charged with bias. If the chair is sincerely committed to serving the whole assembly, he will naturally inform both sides.

One salient rule in the practice of parliamentary procedure is to act in such wise that the chair, for instance, cannot reasonably be charged with bias. Presiding requires the chair to suspend judgment many times, certainly to remain quiet about his opinions. There is recourse for the chair in a ballot that will give his opinion equal value with all other members.

Parliamentary procedure always attempts to balance the rights of the individual member with the rights of the assembly. If an individual member had unlimited scope, no meeting of minds could ensue, and no decisions made. If the assembly had unlimited scope, the individual member would be just a drone in the hive. It is the balance between these two extremes that produces progress. As examples, the individual member always has the right to secure information about the motion on the floor-yet he may not interrupt a vote to find out. The assembly has the right to demand a two-thirds vote for motions that inhibit its right to debate, yet it may not refuse to consider such abridgment of its rights.

"What happens when the chair won't recognize you?" one person asked a noted parliamentarian.

"Stand up and holler until the chair recognizes you," was the answer.

It is not always easy to demand one's rights as a member, but if one does not demand those rights, they can easily be swept up by someone else who will not hesitate to seize them. For instance, the veteran presider who controls a meeting has lost sight of the inherent truth that authority resides in the assembly, that the Chair's purpose is to expedite the business of the assembly fairly and democratically. But like all other greeds, the greed to control the assembly is heady wine, and the greedy presider will pick up and use power that others have carelessly ignored. He may disguise his greed in saying he is doing what is best for the organization, that too much time is lost in useless debate if he fails to control the assembly by strong arm tactics. But what must be remembered is that democratic procedures are not 'efficient," they are, in fact, time consuming and inefficient. But as Churchill said, democracy is an inefficient way of government, but it is so much better than anything else.

Take from the Table

Three of our parliamentary authorities - Robert, Demeter, and Sturgis - discuss Take from the Table. Keesey cannot logically discuss the procedure because he opposes Lay on the Table, a ". . . purpose well served by the motions To Postpone or To Recess."

To Take from the Table is a mirror image of To Lay on the Table: it requires only a second and a majority vote. Take from the Table has precedence over other main motions, that is, if two speakers are asking the chair for recognition, the first to make a new motion, and the second to move to Take from the Table, the second person must be given precedence.

One central characteristic of Take from the Table requires that substantial business intervene between the motions to Lay on the Table (or to Table) and To Take from the Table. For example, if the motion to raise dues has been tabled then after disposal of the dinner dance motion, the tabled motion can be brought again before the assembly by the motion To Take from the Table. A member may not raise a point of order immediately after the tabling of a motion, and then move to Take from the Table.

A tabled motion may also be taken from the table at the next regular meeting of the club, either by a motion from the floor or from the chair. The chair, however, must consider influencing obliquely the importance of the motion tabled by bringing the tabled motion again before the assembly. If the original maker of the motion to table does not move to take the motion from the table, it is debatable whether the chair should do so for him. Sometimes the phrase, "Table to the Next Meeting" is used by the chair. If there is a time specification, the proper motion is "Postpone to the Next Meeting," the chair seeing that the postponed motion is part of the agenda of the next meeting.

In some legislative assemblies to table a motion is to kill it. But Robert et. al. deal with non-legislative assemblies, and with all the parliamentary authorities who recognize the motion, the position is the same: To table is to delay until later in the same meeting or to the next regular meeting. If conditions have changed between meetings so the motion tabled no longer has sufficient support in the assembly, it "falls to the ground," or expires. The procedure to Take from the Table is not just mechanical, based on the passage of time. Its effective use requires convincing a majority to consider anew a postponed motion after having been persuaded by supportive data for taking the motion from the table.

CHAPTER IX - Privileged Motions
Orders of the Day

Privileged motions sit at the top of the order of precedence, meaning, they supersede original main motions, incidental main motions, and subsidiary motions as well as motions that bring a question again before the assembly, and motions not specifically classified in RONR.

The acronym FARPO is generally used by followers of Robert to help memorize the five privileged motions. However, since in the order which the motions have precedence, Call for the Orders of the Day is lowest, and Fix the Time to Which to Adjourn is the highest followed by Adjdourn, Recess, and Question of Privilege, perhaps the acronym should be OPRAF. On the other hand, FARPO is easier to learn, and there is usually little confusion about going backwards, that is, taking the "O" in FARPO *first* because there are only five privileged motions - two of which are quite simple.

Call for the Orders of the Day simply means, "Mr. Chairman, please follow the agenda." The chair usually replies, "The chair stands corrected The next item is #5, not #6," The probability is that the chairman simply erred. Another reason for calling for the orders of the day is to remind the chair that a special order is scheduled to be discussed at a specific time, at 2:15 P.M. At the last regular meeting, a motion was made and passed by 2/3 vote to postpone consideration of dues until the next regular meeting. The "next regular meeting" is the current meeting.

Member: Mr. Chairman, I call for the Orders of the Day. At this time, 2:15 P.M. the special order concerning dues set up at our last regular meeting must be considered.

Chair: The chair thanks the member. The member is correct. We must take up the matter of raising dues next. After the matter of dues is resolved, we will return to the agenda where we left off.

The Call for the Orders of the Day must be carried out at the request of one member, unless 2/3 of the members present vote not to return to the agenda. This call may be made when another has the floor and the call may not be ignored. It would do little good if the maker of the motion calling for the orders of the day had to wait until the item being discussed on the floor was completed. His motion would then have little force, in fact, could not be used. A clumsy or incorrect wording of the motion calling for the Orders of The Day may not be used by the chair as an excuse to avoid returning to the agenda. Robert warns about the Chair's using a picayunish meticulousness of language that masks the chair's desire to control rather than to help. The chair is obligated to help the member formulate what he wants to say so long as the member's *intention* is clear.

What about the member who has the floor when the call is made? He has to realize that certain motions, Call for the Orders of the Day, Parliamentary Inquiry, Point of Order, Point of Information, Division of the Assembly, and Appeal are procedures that may legally interrupt him. Of course the chair must assure that these motions are not abused. If the chair suspects a procedure called for by a member is a ploy used to frustrate the work of the assembly, the chair simply calls the procedure frivolous and rules it out of order. If the person making the motion feels aggrieved, he may appeal the decision of the chair. Then the assembly decides by a majority vote whether it supports the chair or the member.

The member having the floor at the time of the interruption must be protected from unnecessary interruption, but he may not demand to hold the floor when another member has urgent business that must be attended to immediately. It is ludicrous to think that the member holding the floor must not be interrupted when another member wants to notify the chair that a fire has broken out in the back of the assembly hall!

When business commendatory by nature is before the assembly for consideration, the negative vote is not taken. If the motion above had been made from the floor, the negative vote should not be taken out of consideration for the person being commended. Should someone feel aggrieved because the negative note was not taken, he can appeal the decision of the chair not to take the negative vote. Calling for the Orders of the Day, historically speaking, means, "Take up the special orders and the general orders during this meeting." The special orders have time tags attached to them; general orders are taken up during unfinished business.

While it is the obligation of the chair to set up the agenda that included any special or general orders, it is still incumbent on any member to speak up when he knows a mistake is being made. However nervous a member might be about calling for the orders of the day, he may not use nervousness as an excuse after the meeting, saying he was to nervous to speak up. Nervous or not, as a member he is obligated to speak up. Members who fear to speak up frequently feel that those in charge are calm and unassailed by feelings of nervousness or inadequacy. Only in the bathtub can many of us feel completely at ease. In a meeting one does what is *right*. Later one deals with the nervousness.

One hint: If you are nervous in meetings, write out what you want to say, and *read* it when you get the floor. It is better to read than to try to express unsure thoughts through a fog of nervous uncertainty. The goal of fulfilling one's obligation is important; personal comfort is not.

Raise a Question of Privilege

There are five privileged motions: Fix the Time to Which to Adjourn; Adjourn; Recess; Raise a Question of Privilege; and Call for the Orders of the Day. Raise a Question of Privilege, though similar in spelling to Privileged Motion, has its own identification. There are two forms to Questions of Privilege: a question concerning the assembly, and a question concerning a member. Demeter states, "Question of privilege relates in a broad interpretation to the following subjects; the members' Safety, Health, or Integrity, or Protection of their Property, (acronym SHIP)."

Consider a convention of two hundred people. There is a member at the microphone, debating a proposed amendment to the bylaws of the organization.

Member: (Suddenly shouting from the rear without being recognized by the chair.) Mr. Chairman, I raise a question of privilege concerning the assembly.

Chair: What is your question of privilege?

Member: The thunderstorm outside is so great I can't hear the speakers.

Chair: The member's question of privilege is well taken. Will the sergeant-at-arms see that the windows are closed. We will now return to the speaker at the microphone.

Note that the business before the assembly was set aside while the Question of Privilege was disposed of. Immediately after the resolution of the thunderstorm problem, the interrupted business of the assembly was resumed, as if no interruption had occurred.

Another less formal scenario might be: The member at the microphone is interrupted by a voice saying. "We can't hear you because of the storm outside." The chair would then say, "Will the sergeant-at-arms see that the windows are closed." Immediately thereafter the member at the microphone resumes where he left off.

A member rises to complain that the room is cold. The chair resolves the problem with instructions to the appropriate person. Another member complains to the chair about the conversations being held around him. Still another member may rise to a Question of Privilege on the basis of a personal attack on his motives or his honesty. The chair must differentiate between personal attack and attack on another member's ideas. The latter is allowed; the former is not. However, some people identify themselves so closely with their ideas that they may consider any attack upon their ideas as a personal attack upon them. An example of property as the basis for a question of personal privilege is a member's rising to notify the chair that the members' cars in the parking lot are being vandalized by hoodlums.

In all the emergency cases above, immediate action is required However, in another category of Question of Privilege, there is need for deliberate action. Consider the following:

Member: (rising without being recognized) Mr. Chairman, I rise to a Question of Privilege for the assembly.

Chair: What is your question?

Member: Mr. Chairman, what is being discussed is of such personal nature that it should be discussed only with members present.

Chair: The point is well made. The chair requests that our visitors leave at this point. We know you understand that we must handle delicate personal matters in confidence.

The Question of Privilege is decided first, after which the assembly returns to the business interrupted by the call for the Question of Privilege. Should two Questions of Privilege arise at the same time, one dealing with the assembly, the other with a person, the Question of Privilege dealing with the assembly must be resolved first. Since rising to a Question of Privilege stops the assembly business, a Question of Privilege must be used charily. The chair must be sensitive to improper or frivolous use of the procedure. For instance, should a member interrupt another member on a Question of Privilege to ask the cost of the item under debate, the chair disallows the interruption because it is not a Question of Privilege. Tactfully, the chair may say, "What you are asking is important, but it is not a Question of Privilege. Immediately after the member finishes speaking, the chair will call on you."

Demeter recommends that the Question of Privilege called for be allowed if there is doubt that it is a proper Question of Privilege. Would the chair so decide, the decision of the chair can be appealed by a simple, "I appeal the decision of the chair." Should a Question of Privilege be raised when there is no other business before the assembly, it is a main motion, which requires a second, is debatable, amendable, and requires a majority vote for adoption.

Keesey points out that To Raise Question of Privilege and To Rise to a Parliamentary Inquiry" ... are not motions, but procedures for making individual requests for action or information on procedure ... The Point of Order is the most logical refuge for these two obsolete forms, since it allows members to appeal the decision of the chair. Use of the Point of Order to include all these functions is recommended with the understanding that the presiding officer must control the use of a Point of Order, subject to appeal by the assembly."

Following the logical precept that the chair must help members to express what they intend - even though they use confused or inadequate language - the use of Point of Order for Parliamentary inquiry, or Question of Privilege, seems reasonable. All three procedures result in an appealable decision by the chair.

As every member has a right to ask what the question before the house is, so he has a right to raise a question of privilege under appropriate circumstances. There must be a willingness to suffer possible embarrassment on a member's part when challenging the fairness of the chair; otherwise, the member may never make the challenge. Of course the challenge is made in a courteous manner, for the chair may be right - and rude insistence on the part of the member can only multiply the embarrassment that follows being wrong. It is not suggested here that the chair is deliberately unfair, but as eternal vigilance is the price of liberty, so willingness to challenge the chair is the price of a member's full participation.

Recess starts right after its own motion is adopted

Parliamentary authorities explain To Recess in the same basic way, exemplified by Sturgis, who writes, ". . . (to recess is) to permit an interlude in a meeting and to set a definite time for continuing the meeting." The reasons for recess vary widely, ranging from interrupting a three-hour meeting with a prearranged recess, to recessing the meeting for the counting of ballots, for physical comfort, and to free participants from remaining in session while ballots are toted up.

All the authorities stipulate the essential difference between recess and adjournment - time. Keesey, in his succinct style writes, "The motion to recess must stipulate the duration of the recess and thus provide for reconvening the meeting. There is no limit on the length of a recess, as long as it neither extends beyond the time set for the next regular or special meeting nor constitutes an adjournment as in a convention." Here Keesey warns against the misuse of recess. By calling for a recess that extends beyond the scheduled limits of a convention the purpose of recess is subverted, perhaps to adjourn without using the word adjourn, to recess being less extended than adjourn.

Sturgis differentiates between recess and adjourn: "A motion to recess suspends the current meeting until a later time; the unqualified motion to adjourn *terminates* the meeting." Another difference between recess and adjournment is that ". . . the next time the assembly is called to order, the difference is that at the conclusion of a recess there never are any 'opening' proceedings, but business is always immediately resumed where it was left off, just as if there had been no recess." (Robert)

The terms, recess and adjourn, are frequently mixed up. The chairman must differentiate, and carry out what the member *means*, rather than what the member says. Better yet, the chair should clarify aloud what the chair perceives the member proposes, and to ascertain that the chair perceives correctly. Still, Robert points out, "It is common, especially in conventions, to hear the word recess also applied to a longer break that does terminate a meeting, and that consequently should be understood as an adjournment, as in 'to recess until tomorrow'." When Congress takes a "summer recess" it is actually adjourned, the term "summer recess" being a convenient conventional expression.

Interestingly, most of the parliamentary authorities agree on the rules governing recess, the exceptions being Sturgis and Keesey. All agree that Recess:

1. May not interrupt a speaker

2. Requires a second

3. Is amendable

4. Requires a majority vote

Where Sturgis and Keesey disagree is their stipulation that the motion is debatable. Debate is ". . . . being restricted to brief discussion on the time, duration, or need of recess" (Sturgis); and, "Although the motion is not debatable, the mover of the motion To Recess, or of a proposed amendment to it should be permitted to state his reasons for the motion or amendment." (Keesey)

Strictly speaking, amending a motion to recess for ten minutes to fifteen minutes, should be treated as any other amendment, that is, the amendment of 15 minutes should be voted on first, then the amended motion for a recess for fifteen minutes should be voted on. Functionally, members will ordinarily agree on the fifteen minutes, assuming that they are simply approving a recess of fifteen minutes. To demand a vote on the fifteen minutes as a amendment, and with its acceptance, then vote on the amended motion, To Recess, makes no sense in the real world. It is this insistence on form over function that Robert condemns, a pettifoggery that discredits parliamentary procedure. The motion to recess is in order even when a quorum is not present. One purpose of recess is to allow the rounding up of members who would constitute a quorum, and would thus allow the assembly to continue its work.

The motion To Recess comes in two forms: as privileged motion and as main motion. If the motion To Recess is made while another motion is before the assembly, it is privileged. For example,

Member Ready: Mr. Chairman

Chairman: The chair recognizes Mr. Ready.

Member Ready: Mr. Chairman, we have been discussing buying the new word processor for the office for forty-five minutes. I move for a recess for fifteen minutes. The call of nature is strong for some of us, and I need a drink of water.

Chairman: The chair appreciates Mr. Ready's concern for the comfort of all of us. Because his motion for a recess interrupts the motion on the floor, To Recess in this case is a privileged motion; it requires a second, is amendable, and it requires a majority vote. Without objection - and the chair sees none - we stand in recess for fifteen minutes. We will reconvene at precisely 2:45 P.M., and will continue at that point with the motion concerning the word processor.

OR

Mr. Willing: Mr. Chairman.

Chairman: The chair recognizes Mr. Willing.

Mr. Willing: I move for a recess for fifteen minutes.

Chairman: Mr. Wailing's motion is an incidental main motion, and is debatable, amendable, and requires a majority vote because it is moved at a time when there is no other motion before the assembly.

The perceptive chair may propose a motion to recess, perhaps noting the weariness of the members, asking for unanimous consent. The motion to recess can also be made from the floor followed by a second, and a majority vote.

Another good reason for the motion To Recess is to allow sides to rally their forces, to consult, and to plan strategy for the rest of the meeting. Two authorities, Robert and Demeter, disagree on the vote necessary to change a pre-scheduled recess. Robert holds that two thirds of the members present and voting must agree to change the time for the recess whereas Demeter says that a majority vote is sufficient. In most cases, probably, the difference is unimportant for a call for a recess will probably result in a vote nearer unanimity than majority or two-thirds support.

The starting of a recess period is not difficult, for generally a recess takes place immediately after the motion for it is adopted, and members are usually ready for a break. It is at the end of the recess that complications can arise. The chair states, "We will recess for fifteen minutes." But time is flexible for most people, determined by their personal convenience. So, "fifteen minutes" is not enough direction for members. If the chair says, "We will recess for fifteen minutes. It is now 3:35. We will reconvene at 3:50," the chair must rap the gavel at exactly 3:50 P.M., and pick up where the assembly left off before it recessed.

There is a momentum to every well-run meeting. The chair must develop and nurture that momentum reconvening the meeting at 3:50 P.M. - no sooner, no later - showing discipline on the chair's part, and an expectation that members will cooperate. Primarily, it is the unnecessary lags and delays in meetings that undergird the poor reputation meetings have among too many people. A well-run, highly-organized meeting is a joy; an informal, casually run meeting is a bore.

Adjourn - The Happy Parliamentary Procedure

Of all the sounds in a meeting, the most popular is, "The meeting is adjourned." That relief generally follows meetings that are too long, poorly organized, or lack substance. So popular is the motion, that the negative vote rarely needs asking for. Adjourn is the second-highest privileged motion, preceding Recess, Raise a Question or Privilege, and Call for the Order of the Day. Only Fix the Time to Which to Adjourn has precedence over Adjourn.

Interestingly, Robert ignores Adjourn in his order for business, the agenda. (p 34) Sturgis adds to Robert's six items, three more: Call to Order, Announcements, and Adjournment, but ignores special and general orders. (p. 116) Keesey restricts his Order of Business to five items, like Robert, excluding Adjourn. (p. 100) Demeter has the most elaborate Orders of Business, having six of them! In only one of them does he use Adjourn, but in five of them he uses Good of the Order, or a variation. (pp. 20, 21)

Demeter also adds items that the other parliamentary authorities omit, specifically, the opening of the meeting. Prayer, Pledge of Allegiance, a patriotic song - any or all of these may be included before the substantive part of the meeting begins, usually with the reading of the minutes of the previous meeting. It seems puzzling that the parliamentary authorities eliminate Adjourn from their orders of business, their agendas, but the reasoning on the part of these experts is not readily apparent.

Adjourn is made simple: motion, second, no debate, no amending, majority vote - and it is in order much of the time of the meeting. One attorney on Long Island brought suit in court because his motion was not acted on before the meeting was adjourned. Of course the assembly has the authority to quit working when a majority of the members want to quit. The motion to adjourn is designed to determine quickly and simply the wish of the assembly to continue or to terminate.

Functionally, there are two Adjourns: the privileged motion and the main motion. The privileged motion obtains when another motion is before the assembly.

Member A: Mr. chairman, we have been discussing the motion about the summer picnic for an hour. I move adjournment.

Member B: Second.

Chair: It has been moved and seconded that the meeting be adjourned. If there is no objection, and the chair sees none, the meeting is adjourned. (This is Unanimous Consent).

Another, more usual version of Adjourn is:

Chair: It has been moved and seconded that the meeting be adjourned. All in favor say "aye." Those opposed say "nay." The "ayes" have it, the meeting is adjourned.

The motion about the summer picnic "falls to the ground," that is, lost. It can be renewed at the next meeting. A motion to adjourn is always privileged except when it is qualified in any way, as adjourning to a definite time in the future, or when adopted, would dissolve the assembly with no provision for another meeting, as in a mass meeting or the last meeting of a convention." (Robert, p. 233)

Usually, a motion to adjourn simply terminates a meeting held at regular times, say, monthly. The members know there will be a meeting next month, and have no fear that adjournment of the present meeting will dissolve the organization. The qualification referred to above deals with specifying that the present meeting be adjourned to a fixed time in the future - next Tuesday at 2 P.M. - or limits the adjournment of the present meeting in any way.

A mass meeting is a one-time assembly that dissolves when it adjourns. <u>Sine die</u> is used to terminate the meeting of a legislative body; effectively, it is used at the end of a mass meeting, though it is rarely spoken.

At the first meeting of the Chicago City Council under Mayor Washington, adjournment was moved five minutes after the council was convened. Was adjournment legal? Yes, for there is no time limit on the length of a meeting, unless a limit is specified in the by-laws or by pre-arrangement for the meeting.

A motion to adjourn may be made only after recognition by the chair, and may not interrupt the speaker holding the floor. Even after a motion to adjourn has been made, seconded and voiced by the chair, it does not take effect until the chair so orders. For example, between the time the motion is announced by the chair, a person may say something for the "good of the order," or announce a future action, as two examples. The meeting is actually over when the chairman bangs the gavel and announces, "The meeting is over."

And it really is over. Someone may belatedly announce that the assembly must be told something important. While the chair may ask members to stand quietly to listen to the announcement, the chair may not call the assembly back into order to act upon the announcement. In order to consider the announcement, a special meeting must be ordered, with that announcement as the sole agenda item, or the announcement may be included in the agenda of the next regular meeting.

There is one exception: If a member was trying to get the attention of the chair before adjournment was declared by the chair, the chair may call the assembly back into order, but only for the one item. (Robert, 239)

Keesey states, "If business must be considered after the presiding officer has entertained a motion to Adjourn, he may request permission to withdraw the motion, or, having explained the urgency of the situation, may state, 'The chair requests that this urgent matter be attended to before adjournment' and proceed to state the question" (p. 58). The confusion described above is best avoided by slow and careful action by the chair in declaring the meeting adjourned. The chair should declare the meeting adjourned only when sure the assembly wants to adjourn. If in doubt, the chair should wait a few seconds. There must not be haste on the part of the chair to declare the meeting adjourned, -nor may there be the appearance of haste.

Chair: The motion to adjourn has been made and seconded. Is there anything more to come before the assembly? The chair, seeing none, declares this meeting adjourned. (Bangs the gavel.)

The chairman does not sigh, declare "I'm glad that's over!" or in any way give the impression that he has been relieved of a burden. However, the chair may feel inside, such outward expression of inner feelings may irritate those members who wanted the meeting to continue but did not have the courage to vote against adjournment. The chair, being the single most convenient target, will be blamed for railroading by some who lost. It does not matter that the charge is untrue, the chair wants to avoid time-consuming trivial criticism by defanging these tigers, and by taking the extra time before adjournment has been announced, assures that no member is trying to get the attention of the chair.

Axiomatically, the chair presides expecting the unreasonable to happen. It is simple-minded to expect members to show reasonableness, as the chair defines reasonableness. It is in taking time to be sure that no member can reasonably accuse the chair of trying to get the meeting over with that the chair can lessen unfair criticism of the chair's presiding. In presiding, one takes the long way round, that is, one repeats even when one supposes that everyone knows what is happening. But repeating, even for many of those who do know what is happening is reassuring; and such repeating is vital to offset those who will later blame their inattention on the chair.

Presiding is an opportunity and an obligation. Its purpose is to facilitate the business of the assembly. For the chair to expect more than acceptance by the people being served is too idealistic. That the chair is there to serve, is a necessary, almost impersonal, means for completing assembly business. That's not a happy description of the chair, but it's an honest one.

Adjourn meeting to another specific day and time

Fix the Time to Which to Adjourn holds the highest position of the privileged motions, best explained by illustration:

The meeting has run longer than expected. Rather than have the rapidly diminishing number of members present vote on increasing dues, a motion that the whole membership should vote on, Member A addresses the chair:

Chair: The chair recognizes Member A.

Member A: Mr. chairman, I move that when we adjourn, we adjourn this meeting until next Tuesday evening at 8 P.M.

Member B: Second.

Chair: It is moved that when we adjourn, we adjourn until next Tuesday evening at 8 P.M. At that time, we will continue as if there had been no interruption of time in the meeting. Any member may amend the time, but the motion is not debatable. All in favor, say "aye." All opposed, say "nay." The "ayes" have it. When this meeting is adjourned, it will be adjourned until next Tuesday at 8 P.M. The chair recognizes Member A.

Member A: I move adjournment.

Member B: Second.

Chair: All in favor, say "aye." All opposed, say "nay." The "ayes" have it. The meeting is adjourned.

What happened? Member A recognized that the reduced number of members present, fatigue, and eagerness to conclude the meeting combined to make a considered judgment of a dues increase unlikely. Still, he did not want the motion lost, lest it not be renewed at the next meeting. By moving to adjourn the meeting to a specific time in the future he insures the meeting will continue, and the dues motion will be considered.

Though the procedure is rarely used, it is important for it allows added consideration of dues without subjecting the dues motion to the risk of being lost. In some respects, the procedure sets up a special meeting for next Tuesday at 8 P.M. for the consideration of dues. However, additional items may be brought up, for the adjourned meeting is not a special meeting. It is really the same meeting with a long recess between two parts of the meeting.

A most likely scenario in most meetings is:

Member C: Mr. Chairman

Chair: The chair recognizes Member C.

Member C: I move we adjourn till next Tuesday at 8 P.M.

Member D: Second.

While the usual terminology for Fix the time to Which to Adjourn has not been followed, its substance is included in the motion to adjourn. Perhaps the chair should explain about the reading of the minutes of the meeting just adjourned at the beginning of the adjourned meeting, next Tuesday at 8 P.M., but it appears redundant for the chair to stop and require the formal language of Robert from Member C. The difference between the above form of adjournment and the privileged motion to adjourn is pivotal. Setting a time for an adjourned meeting allows amending that time, whereas the privileged motion to adjourn, seconded, and announced by the chair requires only a majority vote.

It is significant how differently the parliamentary authorities consider Fix the Time to Which to Adjourn. Keesey finds the motion objectionable. "There is no need for this awkwardly stated motion which is almost never used outside of instructional meetings in parliamentary procedure . . . If it is necessary to set a time for the next meeting, the motion To Recess until (stating the date and time) meets the need (p86). Demeter merely lists the procedure without comment. Robert adds, "at the adjourned meeting, except for the reading of the minutes, business will be taken up from the point at which the previous meeting adjourned . . ." (p210). The principal responsibility falls on the chair who must determine what the maker of the motion is actually trying to say, that is, for the time for an adjourned meeting or adjournment.

CHAPTER X - Incidental Motions
Incidental motions - An Overview

Of the twenty-five incidental motions listed in the tinted pages of Robert's latest revision, only one, "Duty, to be excused from" is both debatable and amendable. All the rest are not debatable; nine are amendable. It is obvious that allowing debate on incidental motions could so bog the assembly down in discussing the incidental motion that the main motion could become lost. The reasons for allowing amendments are manifold and uniquely different:

1. To call for ballot vote.

2. To consider a series individually or as a whole.

3. To ask for a standing vote.

4. To make two motions out of a double motion.

5. To fix time for a motion to take effect.

6. To close nominations.

7. To reopen nominations.

8. To make motions relating to nominations (except #6, or #7 above).

9. To make motions relating to voting while subject is pending.

When there is a vote, a ballot vote is in order. The ballot vote has several advantages:
1. It allows members to vote in complete privacy, the vote of the chair being intermixed with all other ballots.
2. It relieves anxiety of people who fear to vote their convictions visibly for fear of other persons.
3. It is the most democratic form of voting.

Sometimes a series of resolutions can be voted on as a whole, if there is no objection. If presented as a whole the assembly may vote on them as a whole, or vote to consider them separately. If it appears they will be presented separately, they can be presented as a whole. The separate parts do not become separate motions, as in division of a question, but are voted on in series, *seriatim.*

In calling for a division of the house, the individual member is demanding a standing vote of the members. However, the call for a standing vote is not a call for a standing *counted* vote, a procedure that might become cumbersome in a large assembly. However, on an important matter, a standing counted vote may be the best count because accurately judging the number of ayes and nays may become suspect when only sizes of the groups are compared. Counting the ayes and nays of the standing members, tabulating and recording the votes, cannot be faulted as a procedure in important matters, and may save much time and trouble later.

Suppose a garden club wants to vote an increase in dues in May before members start vacationing in June, with the stipulation that the dues not take effect until the new fiscal year begins in

September. While the motion to increase dues is pending, a member moves to have the dues increase take place in September. The incidental motion thus becomes a part of the amended motion to increase dues.

At any time during the nominations process a member may move to close nominations, a motion that requires 2/3 vote for adoption. However, the Chair must be sure that the motion has the necessary 2/3 support for a member may move to close nominations too early in order to cut off competition for his nominee. With unanimous consent, the Chair may declare nominations closed. To reopen nominations is simple, requiring only a majority vote, allowing no debate, but allowing amending. It is axiomatic that the right of the assembly to debate and decide is made easy while the removal of the right of the assembly to debate and decide requires a 2/3 vote.

A motion related to nominations is simple: not debatable, but amendable, requiring a majority vote. For example, if the Nominations Committee has presented its slate, and the Chair has asked for nominations from the floor - as it must - then a member may move to have the names of all the nominees read to the assembly. The Chair must comply. If the Chairs does not, a member may appeal the decision of the chair by repeating his motion, and then appealing to the assembly when the Chair rules his motion out of order.

One obvious use is to move for a ballot, if made while the nominations are pending. There should be no hesitation to move for a ballot on the part of members, nor to make other motions concerning nominations, such as a motion to have the results of the upcoming election reported to the members near the end of the current meeting.

Appeals - All Kinds

All our four parliamentary authorities, Robert, Sturgis, Keesey, and Demeter explain appeal to the decision (ruling) of the chair. But only Robert has two kinds of appeal, and three variations of the second appeal. All recognize that the assembly has recourse from error or arbitrariness of the Chair. Without such recourse, the Chair could become tyrannical, and parliamentary procedures could become history.

Robert (p. 257) argues that disagreeing with a ruling of the chair is ". . . no more delicate than disagreeing with another member in debate." In my experience, it's much more difficult to disagree with a ruling of the Chair than to disagree with another member, but delicacy and personal comfort are not the motivating forces. If the Chair is in error, that error must be pointed out, uncomfortable though that pointing out may be to the member. Correctness in the meeting must prevail, and error must be eliminated, no matter its source.

Robert (p. 257-8) states, "No appeal can be made from the chair's response to an inquiry . . . since such a reply is an opinion," not a ruling . . . For example, if, in answer to a parliamentary inquiry, the chair states that a certain motion would be out of order at the time, this reply is not subject to appeal. "However, by making a motion of the point of order denied by the Chair, the Chair must make a ruling that the motion is our of order. His ruling can then be appealed and a majority of the members must vote with the Chair to sustain the ruling of the Chair."

Suppose a member asks the chair if a motion to adjourn is out of order and the chair says it is, the opinion of the Chair may not be appealed. The member then moves adjournment. When the Chair rules the motion to adjourn out of order, the ruling of the Chair can then be appealed to the assembly. If the Chair is sustained, the appeal fails. If the Chair is not sustained, the appeal succeeds and the Chair must reverse its ruling.

It is not to be assumed that the Chair errs deliberately or for personal gain. The Chair may make an honest error. For example, if the Chair declares a motion adopted when a member thinks the motion has been defeated, then the member appeals the ruling of the Chair. An appeal is not an attack on the Chair, but a motion to secure the truth. A more expeditious and equally valid route is to call out "Division," thus requiring the Chair to take a standing vote.

A clearer example of appeal is the chair's declaration, for instance, "You may ask questions about the motion, but you may not amend it." Obviously, this opinion of the chair is arbitrary, and erroneous. Any original main motion may be debated and amended - and this presiding president may have known that fact; but he played upon the ignorance of his fellow members, and set up rules for his own personal convenience. Since the Chair has given only an opinion, there is no appeal. But should a member attempt to debate, and the Chair rules debate out of order, then the member may appeal the ruling of the Chair. The assembly then decides whether it will allow debate.

Demeter (p. 127) spells out examples of deviation from proper procedure by the chair:

1. ". . . if the Chair misassigns the floor or incorrectly recognizes a member, such as if he gave the floor to B when A should have been recognized;"

2. ". . . if the Chair rules on a motion as not within the scope of the organization's purposes;"

3. ". . . when the Chair rules on the germaneness of a motion;"

4. ". . . when he rules on points or order and questions of privilege;"

5. The Chair entertains a motion of lower rank over a pending motion of higher rank because he does not respect the rank of motions. For example, once a motion on the floor has been made and seconded that the pending motion be considered at the next meeting (Postpone to a Certain Time), the Chair may not allow a motion (To Refer to Committee) be considered.

While a member should not hesitate to bring an appeal, he must bring the appeal with courtesy, without implication that the Chair has made a mistake deliberately or is so ignorant of parliamentary procedure that he must be corrected sharply. The axiom that one applies no more pressure than the situation calls for is a good one. One can always use more pressure if the amount initially applied does not work; but if one kills a fly with a baseball bat, he also damages the table on which the fly sat.

Many of the above difficulties can be resolved by a Point of Order from the floor. The Point of Order may interrupt the speaker, and must be dealt with immediately.

It is a tight line to walk in meetings, but one must be serious, not grim; formal, not arrogant. One must assume one's fellows are honest until proven otherwise. They are subject to misjudgments, which are not lies. What is a lie? A lie is a deliberate conflict between what the speaker knows and what he says. The person who misspeaks from ignorance or misinformation is not a liar, he is just mistaken. Therefore, in parliamentary debate, one stresses what one knows to be true, combats error, and pushes for resolution of differences by vote of the assembly.

Earlier I recommended the setting of ground rules for meetings. Prominent among those rules is the requirement that all members refrain from attacking motives of others, to confine themselves to arguing facts and positions. That requisite for common courtesy leads to the second type of appeal advanced only by Robert: "Appeal, relating. to indecorum or transgression of rules of speaking, or to the priority of business, or if made while an unbeatable question is pending". (Robert, t. 10)

When one member demands of another member, "Why did you vote that way?" he breaks two parliamentary rules: No one is required to defend or explain his vote, and the motives of another member may not be questioned. What that member says may be attacked vigorously, but the person and/or his motives may not be impugned. One may call a member's ideas "idiotic," but one may not call a member an "idiot."

Robert's "priority of business" can easily be secured by a member's calling for the Orders of the Day, the Agenda.

Member: Mr. Chairman, you skipped item 3 on the agenda."

Chair: The Chair is in error, and apologizes. The proper item of business at this time is item 3 on the agenda.

An appeal ". . . if made while any undebatable question is pending" is explained by Robert's *Parliamentary Law* (p. 152), "When an undebatable question is pending, its decision should not be delayed by interjecting a debatable one."

Perhaps the above can be explained by other incidental motions that are not debatable. No debate is allowed in incidental motions because the debate of a motion could become protracted endlessly if the motion to decide if a motion is debatable can itself be debated. For example, if the incidental motion to suspend the rules is itself debated, the decision to suspend the rules can become bogged down so much that the motion to be suspended is not voted on. The non-debate of incidental motions is inherent in the term, incidental motion, a motion incidental to the motion before the house.

One is reminded also that there may be only primary and secondary amendments to a motion because a tertiary motion could make the consideration of the motion so involved that clear debate could become impossible for many members.

Questions & Answers

1. Every meeting the president of our garden club adjourns, she adjourns the meeting without asking anyone else. Is she right?
Yes and no. Yes if she looks around the room and determines no one is asking for the floor. Even then she should ask, "Is there any further business? There being none, the meeting is adjourned." No, if she decides on her own, without asking members if that is their wish, the members having the final authority.

2. At the last meeting of our condo, I voted no on the motion to decrease our reserve. This woman, whom I don't even know, turned to me and asked, "Why did you vote no? Do you think you know better than the rest of us?" What should I have done?
You should have risen to a Point of Order (of Personal Privilege) and said, "Madam Chairman, my vote on the last motion has been rudely challenged. I appeal to the chair." The knowledgeable chairman will say, "Every member's vote is private, and may not be challenged. Please do not challenge anyone's vote again."

3. At every meeting of our condo Dolores and Lily sit behind me and gab throughout the meeting. I don't dare to speak to them because they would become so vicious to me. Is there anything I can do?
Yes, appeal to the chair, saying, "Madam President, I cannot hear the speaker. Do we have a mike?" or, "There is so much talking back here I can't hear the speaker."

4. How can I tactfully ask the chair if a ruling of the chair is correct?
Say, "Mister President, before today I had not heard of stopping debate without a vote of the members. Am I right that the members must vote to stop debate?"

Appeal

Demeter states, "Appeals confuse members more than any other parliamentary proceeding . . ." (p. 128). Part of the confusion arises from the two forms of appeal: appeal from a ruling of the chair, and the other, substantially, appeal from perceived improper actions of fellow members.

Most appeals stem from decisions of the chair. An appeal from the decision of the chair is unique in its nature:
1. After a seconded appeal from the floor, the chair has the right to speak first, to defend his discussion.
2. After debate, during which each member is confined to speaking only once, the chair may speak again.
3. The chair asks, "Is the decision of the chair the decision of the assembly?" A majority vote is required to sustain the decision of the chair. Demeter (p. 128) provides alternatives to the formal language above by allowing, "Is the chair right?" and "Is the chair's ruling right?"
4. The motion is not amendable. Probably on the basis that too much time can be used amending the appeal rather than debating the chair's decision.
5. The adoption or rejection of the appeal can be reconsidered, but such reconsideration gets into deep waters of parliamentary procedure. However, the chair should know the reconsiderability of appeal - and hope it never has to use that knowledge!

Three good examples of appeal from the ruling of the chair are:

The chair states, "The motion to buy the new typewriter is not debatable." Members A & B appeal the decision of the chair. The chair then defends its position; there is general debate; and the chair, after speaking again - if it wants - says, "Is the decision of the chair the decision of the assembly?" and then calls for a vote of the assembly (Demeter, p. 128).

Robert points out in "Appropriateness of Appeal. If a member disagrees with a ruling of the chair affecting any substantial question, he should not hesitate to appeal." (p. 257). While what Robert writes is objectively true, it is still easier for most members to disagree with a fellow member than with the chair. The member who notes error on the part of the chair must, in Shakespeare's words, " . . . screw your courage to the sticking place," and speak up. It is better to speak up and be in error than it is to be silent and suffer the stomach rumblings on the ride home that can follow not speaking one's mind.

Sturgis (p. 85) stresses that a member may not appeal a statement of fact by the chair; that is, the member may not appeal the result of a vote. In that case the member can simply say, "Division," and a count of the assembly must be made. Nor may a member use the appeal procedure frivolously, thereby thwarting the prompt and proper execution of the business of the assembly. If the chair so perceives two members' motions and seconds, the chair says, "The case is so plain that the chair cannot entertain the appeal."

Another example of appeal from the decision of the chair is that of the germane amendment: The seconded motion on the floor is to buy a new desk for the clubhouse. One member moves to add the amendment, "and to paint the office green" (Demeter, p. 127). The chair correctly rules the amendment is not germane. The member appeals. Eventually, the members will vote to sustain the chair's decision or to reject it. If the members reject the chair's decision, holding that " . . . to paint the office green is germane to the original motion to buy a new desk, the amendment is germane, "the body has the final say" (Demeter, p. 128).

The other appeal relates to ". . . indecorum or transgression of rules of speaking" (Robert, p. 10). This procedure actuates the right of a member to be free of personal attack on his motives or his person. There must be a clear differentiation between the speaker's ideas and his persona. His ideas are always subject to debate, refutation, even scorn. On the other hand, the speaker must not identify himself with his ideas to the extent that he considers any attack upon his ideas as a personal assault upon him. In this appeal, the motion is limited to seconding, and majority vote. Example:

Member B: Mr. Chairman, Member A made the motion because he hopes to get the contract to re-roof the clubhouse.

Member A: I appeal to the chair. Member B has attacked my integrity and honesty.

Chair: The appeal is justified. Member B may oppose the re-roofing of the clubhouse, but he may not challenge the motives of Member A.

Robert (p. 10-T) considers the appeal applicable for "the priority of business," a variation of calling for the Orders of the Day, which is just an elaborate way of saying, "Stick to the agenda, Mr. Chairman." One can envision an appeal to move parts of the agenda around, but this appeal route is rarely used. However, it is a legitimate use of the appeal procedure, and must be acknowledged.

Only Robert deals extensively with Appeal, for only he has the second type appeal. Keesey, Demeter, and Sturgis all deal solely with appeal from the decision of the chair. One supposes that the second case, particularly appeal against personal attack by the speaker, can be handled with Point of Order, and Point of Personal Privilege. Also, if rules for the meeting require speaking only to the motion on the floor, then the chair can stop the speaker by pointing out the error of the speaker.

Sturgis (p. 87) specifies rules that cannot be suspended:

a. Rule stated in statute or charter.
b. Rule of ". . . common parliamentary law such as rules governing notice, quorum, vote requirements, and voting methods."
c. Rule in the bylaws that does not permit its own suspension.

Therefore, an appeal to the above cannot be considered. Even a vote of the assembly to permit such an appeal is not permissible.

There is the story of the member who moved that the bylaws be suspended so a mail ballot could be taken. The motion was seconded, and adopted by majority vote. One knowledgeable member stood and requested the lights be turned out and everyone go home. When asked why he suggested such a silly thing he replied, "You have suspended the bylaws. Without bylaws, there can be no organization. Therefore, since we have no organization, we might as well go home."

One obvious example of use of appeal follows the decision of the chair that a motion has been adopted on a close voice vote. The most expeditious procedure to use is "Division," said by any member, without recognition by the chair. The chair could have avoided this contretemps by saying, "The chair is in doubt. Without objection, there will be a standing counted vote. The chair, seeing no objections, rules that a standing, counted vote will be taken. Tellers, please take your posts." The chair then proceeds to take a standing counted vote. If the majority is in the affirmative, the chair's decision is sustained. If the majority is in the negative, the chair's decision is rejected, and the motion is defeated.

Demeter (p. 131) gives a revealing, and amusing, example of the use - and misuse - of appeal.

Member B: Mr. Chairman, what vote adopts adjournment?

Chair: Majority vote.

Member B: I appeal from your decision. It requires a 2/3 vote.

Chair: The appeal cannot be entertained. The rule says majority.

Member C: Madame Chairman, how many delegates can we elect?

Chair: Article nine states: 'nine delegates shall be elected.'

Member C: Madame Chairman, I move that we elect eleven instead.

Chair: The motion is out of order; it violates the bylaw.

Member C: Madame Chairman, I appeal from your ruling.

Chair: The appeal is out of order; the bylaw is inviolable.

Member E: Mr. Chairman, how many months has the year?

Chair: Twelve.

Member E: I appeal from your ruling; it has eleven months.

Chair: (calmly and patiently) The appeal is out of order. The calendar says twelve months.

Requests and Inquiries

The four principal parliamentary authorities, Robert, Sturgis, Demeter, and Keesey, deal with requests and inquiries, each differing markedly from the others: Robert's treatment is extensive; Sturgis and Demeter follow with less extensive treatment, and Keesey mentions requests and inquiries not at all.

Those old enough to remember the McCarthy Hearings in Washington in the early 1950's can recall Senator McCarthy's repeated call, "Point of order, Mr. Chairman, point of order." McCarthy's repeated call - from the hindsight of four decades - indicates poor chairmanship on the part of the presider. McCarthy's request demanded immediate attention by the chair, and the fact that McCarthy had to repeat his request so many times is a criticism of the chair, not of McCarthy.

What are these parliamentary requests? Robert gives an excellent list (p. 72):
1. Parliamentary Inquiry - (a request for the chair's opinion on a matter of parliamentary procedure as it relates to the business at hand - not involving a ruling.)
2. Point of information - an inquiry affecting the business at hand.
3. Request to modify or withdraw a motion - after it has been stated by the chair.
4. Request to read papers.
5. Request to be excused from a duty.
6. Request for any other privilege - contrasted to privileged motions.

Parliamentary requests and inquiries grow out of the business of the assembly. As incidental motions they are neither debatable nor amenable, except for Request to be Excused from a Duty, which is both debatable and amenable. A parliamentary inquiry, which bears on a matter of parliamentary law or procedure, is directed to the Chair. An example:

Member: I rise to a point of parliamentary inquiry.

Chair: The member will state the inquiry.

Member: Is it in order at this time to move the previous question? (Robert, p.285)

A point of information seeks information concerning the business at hand, but not related to parliamentary procedure. When addressed to the chair, or through the chair to a member, a point of information is treated immediately.

Member: I rise to a point of information (or, point of information, please)

Chair: The member will state the point (or What is the point?)

Member: The motion calls for a large expenditure. Will the treasurer state the presence balance? (Robert, p. 286)

A member may seek recognition of the chair even when another member is speaking may also ask speaker a question. The speaker allows or does not allow an interruption. If he allows an interruption, the time used by the questioner is taken from the time allotted the speaker. Even though the speaker allows the interruption, speaking to the chair, he and the questioner may not hold a two-way conversation. Each member must address only the chair.

Request to modify or withdraw a motion is simple and logical, but too frequently used can cause confusion. The maker of a motion may withdraw a motion before it has been announced by the chair. However, once the seconded motion has been announced by the chair, the motion belongs to the assembly, and may not be withdrawn except by permission of the assembly.

In a convention in Atlanta, a committee chairman moved the adoption of the recommendations of the committee. When there was a negative reaction from the floor, the committee chairman said, "Okay, I'll change the recommendation." The parliamentarian pointed out to the presider that because the motion for acceptance of the committee's recommendations was now before the assembly, only the assembly could authorize amendment of the motion before the assembly. The chair asked for unanimous consent, received it, and the recommendations were modified as proposed by the chairman of the committee.

The second member may have made an amendment to the motion in the usual way, stating he wanted to amend the motion, and stating his amendment. If the amendment was in order, and was seconded, the amendment would be placed before the assembly. If the amendment passed, it would become part of the original motion, and the assembly would vote on the amended motion.

Though insistence of a member that he be allowed to read a speech into the record is rare, there is provision prohibiting the member from reading sections of a paper. He should properly ask for permission of the chair, who in turn asks permission of the assembly for the member to read excerpts. The member must respect the limited right he has to read excerpts. However, if he does not, then any member may object to his continued reading at any time. The chair would then make a ruling, or the chair may secure a majority vote from the assembly.

A speaker may not ask to read a paper before the assembly. The paper must be made available to the members. For clarification, particularly after debate and amendment, a member may correctly ask that the paper be read again before a vote is taken. However, should a member be absent when the first reading was made, he may not ask for a second reading on the basis of his absence. While he is deprived, it is not proper that the convenience of an individual supersede the convenience of the assembly (Robert, pp 289-91).

The request to be excused from a duty falls into two categories: an essential and a non-essential duty. If the duty is essential to the ongoing of the organization, then the person may not be excused. For instance, the treasurer may not be excused from making periodic financial reports. Should a member not be able to fulfill the obligations of a position he holds, such as attending the number of meetings required in the bylaws, then the member may ask for an excuse from the assembly. Should a member fail to satisfy duties inherent in the position he has accepted, then he should resign.

When I was in New York, I met with the director of the New England region for an organization. Together we set up a workshop, to be held in two months. We wrote to the vice president in charge of continuing education, describing what we intended to do, and asking for some financial support, as authorized in the then current budget. We did not hear from the vice president. Nor could we get a response from the executive board. Later I learned that the vice president did not respond because " . . . her husband was ill." Note that the vice president did not resign, even though she could not carry out the responsibilities of the office to which she had been elected. While it was unfortunate that her husband was ill, that was no excuse for neglecting a regional conference. It is difficult to understand the reason that the vice president could not do both: Take care of her husband, and support the regional conference, particularly since the organization was attempting to broaden its services to its members, and was seeking additional members.

One challenging question is sometimes used on qualifying parliamentary examinations: The president of an organization storms out of a meeting, shouting, "I quit!" Has the president resigned? No, because his resignation must be in writing. The serious matter of resignation requires more formal notification than the shouted resignation of an angry person.

At a Long Island meeting of a four-county organization, the parliamentarian was told that W.C. McLaughlin always made a ten-minute speech near the end of every meeting. The parliamentarian responded, "Why? On what basis does he make this speech?"

"Oh, he just always does it," was the response.

"He has no greater right than any other person to make a ten-minute speech."

For the first time in the memory of many people present, McLaughlin did not make a speech. Perhaps the presence of a qualified parliamentarian at the head table stopped him, for there was organization at the head table that had not been there before. Perhaps he knew he had no such right. At any rate, McLaughlin did not try, and the Chair was spared ruling against him.

Any other request must meet the criterion of urgency, especially if another has the floor. While the assembly has the authority to let whom it wishes speak, the request to speak while another has the floor must be made only in extraordinary circumstances. Heavy smoke is ample reason for interrupting the speaker.

Parliamentary procedure always seeks one goal: to help the assembly reach its legitimate objectives, while protecting the rights of the minority, and those of the individual. The assembly must be prevented from becoming an oppressive body or a rubber stamp. It was said that under Hitler, the Reichstag was the world's largest paid cheering section. On the other hand, a strong-willed individual must not be allowed to abduct the rights of the assembly by lessening the rights of other members. It is in the balance of power between the two loci of power that progress is made.

Suspend the Rules

The local congressman on Long Island accepted the invitation to address a local Rotary Club - but he did not expect to sit through a routine business meeting before his talk! Further, he had another appointment to see some orphans - as he repeatedly told the chairman. The chairman continued with routine business, unruffled and unmoved.

Woodrow Wilson's grandson accepted the invitation to address the Wisconsin Elementary School Principals Association in it annual convention. He said, "If I may speak early in the meeting, I will be able to get a plane out of here tonight. Otherwise, I will have to stay overnight." The chairman continued with routine business, later harumphing, "He had to wait his turn."

No one knew what to do to have the congressman make his talk without delay, and then return to routine business; nor did the elementary principals know what to do. The answer is simple: Suspend the Rules.

Suspend the Rules is an incidental motion that requires only two-thirds vote, without debate its purpose is to set aside the less important for the more important, letting the congressman talk instead of slavishly following an easily rearranged agenda of routine business. Suspend the Rules is not debatable because it is an incidental motion and is incidental to the motion to which it is attached. Were it debatable much assembly time would be taken up deciding the incidental motion while the main motion remains untouched. The non-debatability of incidental motions is reminiscent of the prohibition of tertiary amendments to main motions.

Main motion: The club will have a dinner dance.
Primary amendment: The dinner dance will be held May 5th.
Secondary amendment: The dinner dance will start at 6 P.M. .
Tertiary amendment: Not allowed because there would be too much for members to consider in making decisions about the dinner dance.

Parliamentary procedure has developed over a period of some eight centuries. It stands to reason that procedures have been tried and abandoned, tried and modified, tried and kept. Since the primary purpose of parliamentary procedure is aiding members of an assembly to determine what they want to decide, and since members have been meeting in assembly for centuries, there has been need for winnowing what can easily become unclear verbiage.

Keesey has used his hatchet to drag out and destroy every motion for which he cannot find easy justification, being an energetic pruner of arcane and impertinent procedures. His approach is "Why keep it?" rather than, "Why not keep it?"

Suspend the Rules also exemplifies the parliamentary principle that any limiting of the assembly's right to debate must be supported by a two-thirds vote of the assembly.

If a unanimous vote were required for suspending the rules, it might well not pass because one or two members could thwart the will of the majority by voting no, in effect, making themselves controllers of the assembly. On the other hand, some motions are too important to pass by a simple majority vote, for the fundamental right of the assembly to debate is being removed. Thus, a compromise of two-thirds, a choice between unanimity and majority vote is reasonable.

After the rules have been suspended, an anachronism that means, "Let's suspend the agenda until we can get this other business done," the meeting re-starts where it left off. It is well for the presider or the secretary to note what the motion under debate before the suspension was, and which member held the floor. The need to suspend comes up rarely, but it is pivotal when it does arise.

Parliamentary procedures, like computers, are a part of our lives. Our choice is to know and use them, or have others use them for us.

Creating and Filling Blanks

Even before the annual budget meeting of the Garden Club began, there was a buzz of excitement among its thirty members because the club had decided to buy a computer for its office. For weeks there had been the ebb and flow for buying a computer. Typical remarks were: "We're too small a club to need a computer" countered by, "We're too big a club <u>not</u> to have one. We're losing money by not keeping better track of our expenses." Finally the time had come for the club to decide about the computer.

Mrs. Petzen: I move we buy a computer for our club.

Mr. Petzen: I second.

Chair: It has been moved and seconded that our club buy a computer. Is there any discussion?

Ms. Corrente: I want to buy a computer, but what kind? and how much will we spend?

Chair: Ms. Corrente brings up two questions: what kind of computer, and how much will we spend. Is there further discussion?

Mr. Michael: Who knows anything about computers? I lay tile. But I don't want my money spent by someone who doesn't know any more about computers than I do.

Chair: A point well made, Mr. Michael. Since there are really two considerations here: the purchase of a computer, and the kind of computer to buy. The Chair points out there is a third factor: how much will be spent for the computer? Since there is general support for the purchase of a computer, with reservations about kind and expense, the Chair recommends that a committee of three be set up to determine cost and kind, and report back at the next regular club meeting.

Mr. Legalism: This is our annual budget meeting. By our bylaws we must set up a budget provision for the computer tonight.

Mrs. Bossy: There you go again, Hank, putting road blocks in the way of progress. Madam Chairman, isn't there some way we can handle this business quickly?

Chair: Yes, there is. Our club can agree on the maximum amount of money it wants to spend for the computer. That amount can be set up in the budget. Then a committee of three people can be set up, and make its recommendations at the next regular meeting of our club.

Ms. Corrente: But we have three decisions to make: if we want to buy a computer, what kind it will be, and how much we want to pay for it. How will you handle that, Madam Chairman?

Chair: The club can make two of those decisions now: first, to determine how much to spend. After that decision is made, if the club wants to buy a computer at all. The Petzen motion is the pending motion. If there is no objection, the chair will create a blank as an amendment to that motion, stating, 'I move that we buy a computer at a cost not to exceed $ _____ .'

Ms. Corrente: But what goes in the blank?

Chair: That is what we must decide. In one sense filling that blank is like making nominations: You speak out the amount you think should be spent, that amount will be written on our easel paper.

We will vote on each amount, and the amount that gets a majority will be the amount of money entered in the blank. Everyone understand?

Ms. Corrente: If I understand correctly, I'll say not to exceed $5,000

Other voices: No more than $3,000, $4,000, $1,000, $500.

Chair: The secretary has written the five amounts on the easel paper. The Chair will ask for a vote on these five suggested amounts. All those in favor of $5,000 raise your hands. Two votes. All those in favor of $4,000, raise your hands. Seven votes. All those in favor of $3,000, raise your hands. Seventeen votes. Therefore, the motion will read to buy a computer at a cost not to exceed $3,000.

Mr. Excitable: Wait a minute. What are you trying to pull? Why didn't you vote on the other amounts?

Chair: I didn't ask for a vote on the other amounts because there was no point to calling for the vote. A majority of the members present and voting decided on the $3,000 figure. If the amended motion passed, you may nominate three people to serve on the committee. (Several people: You pick them.)

Chair: Very well, if there is no objection. You voted on the maximum amount you will authorize for the purchase of a computer, if you vote to buy a computer. Now before you goes the amended motion that we buy a computer at a price not to exceed $3,000. Are you ready for the question. All in favor raise your hands. Put your hands down, please. All opposed raise your hands. Put your hands down please. The vote, confirmed by the secretary, is 18 in favor, 12 opposed. The motion is passed. The committee to bring back recommendations at the next regular meeting are: Chairman CC Corrente, Mr. Legalism, and Ms. Noteworthy.

Mr. Obstruct: Does that motion take a 2/3 vote?

Chair: No.

Mrs. Difficult: Why did you appoint only people who favor buying a computer? Why didn't you appoint someone opposed?

Chair: This is a special committee. According to our parliamentary authority, a special committee must be composed of people who favor their assignment. It is in standing committees that different points of view must be represented. There being no other business - and the Chair sees no one asking for the floor - the meeting is adjourned.

The alternative to creating and filling blanks is a complicated series of motions with primary amendments and substitute motions. A motion with $5,000 in the main motion, with a primary amendment that attempts to substitute $1,000 for the $5,000, both of which are defeated, leads inevitably to more main motions and substitute motions until the final decision of $3,000 maximum expenditure is authorized. This hit-and-miss approach is fraught with easily made mistakes, and confusion for the members. Creating and filling blanks is like a garden refreshed with rain after the frustration of watering with a garden hose.

Questions and Answers

1. If creating and filling blanks are such good procedures, how is it I've never heard of them before?
Yours is not an unusual experience. Many people have not heard of the two procedures. But I'll bet you can see the value of them now.

2. Why did you start with the biggest figure first? Why not start with the smallest figure?
Voting for the smallest figure would cause confusion between the cost of the computer and the amount members wanted to pay. The members prefer to pay $500, but for that price they would not get a computer. The rule of thumb is: in buying, start with the least likely figure, probably the highest. In selling, start with the least likely figure, probably the lowest.

3. Instead of the chair's proposing to set up a blank, could this motion come from a member?
Absolutely, may even be better. The member's motion would be seconded, and, if desired, debated.

Objection to the Consideration of a Question

Robert (p. 265) writes, "The purpose . . . is to enable the assembly to avoid a particular original main motion altogether when it believes it would be strongly undesirable for the motion even to come before the assembly."

At first blush, one's reaction is a suspicion that free speech is being manacled, that the right of the assembly to discuss is being denied. Why should the assembly not be able to discuss what it wants? Who has the right to deny the assembly its basic right to discuss and vote?

An example may serve well here. Suppose Congresswoman Eileen Springer is so popular that a motion is made and adopted that the Audubon Garden Club endorse her re-election bid. Later the attorney for the club points out to the president that it is illegal for a not-for-profit organization to endorse a political candidate, that doing so endangers its tax-exempt status. In this situation the assembly would surely move to rescind the adopted motion.

Consider this situation:

Chair: The chair recognizes George Moore.

George: I move to have this club endorse the re-election of Eileen Springer for Congress.

Chair: Is there a second? (Two members rise.)

Frank: (without being recognized by the Chair) I object to the consideration of the question because it's against the law.

Strangely, no defense or justification for the motion can be made by the maker, nor questioning by the other members, but it seems reasonable for the maker to add the five-word phrase to justify his objection, "because it's against the law." Otherwise, members would be asked to vote solely on the thinking of one member who moved the objection, without knowing what his thinking is.

As in other motions, the maker of a motion may add a phrase for clarification while making the motion. Such a phrase is not considered discussion.

The voting is tricky. Those *agreeing* with Frank who object to the consideration of the motion must vote in the negative. Not only must Frank get two-thirds of the members to agree with a motion that has not been discussed, he must get them to vote immediately.

Perhaps, a clearer example is this:

Chair: The Chair recognizes Selma Gordon.

Selma: I move that George Krasner be required to explain his actions last Saturday night.

Anita: I object to the consideration of the question.

Most members would agree that putting George into such an embarrassing position without notice is unfair; he would have no time to prepare a defense. While a written charge can be presented against George, it cannot fairly be brought in the abrupt manner shown above.

A positive vote of less than 1/3, and a negative vote of 2/3, means the objection to the consideration of the question is adopted. The motion concerning George Krasner's actions may not be considered at that time. A positive vote of more than 1/3, and a negative vote of less than 2/3 means the objection to the consideration of the question is defeated. Thereafter, the original motion becomes the pending question, subject to the usual requirements of main motions.

One person has initiated the objection to the consideration of the question, without being recognized by the Chair. But that unusual authority of a single member is offset by the requirement that 2/3 of the vote must agree with that member to sustain the objection. Should the assembly disapprove the objection to the consideration of the question by voting aye, that vote may not be reconsidered. Should the assembly approve the objection to the consideration of the question ". . . two-thirds against consideration sustains objection" (Robert, t 21), that negative vote *may be* reconsidered by a majority vote of the assembly.

Generally, objection to the consideration of a question has such personal overtones that consideration of the question would leave a residual of embarrassment to an individual, if not harm his reputation. In George's case, the charge should be considered only after formal charges have been levied against him, he has been given them in writing, and he has had time to prepare a defense.

Questions and Answers

1. Do you mean I'm supposed to learn these kooky procedures?
If you ignore learning the procedures, someone who has learned them has an advantage over you. While reconsider and enter on the minutes and objection to the consideration of a question are very rarely used, you should be aware of their existence. Also, you will hobble yourself by failure to learn the phrases used frequently in meetings. I think the phrases should be brought up to date. And so does Ray Keesey in his book *Modern Parliamentary Procedures*. Also, I use "Close Debate and Vote" instead of "Call for the Previous Question" when I can. Every conscientious parliamentarian wants to help people to decide what they want to decide, using parliamentary procedures as aids, not barriers.

2. Why not be blunt and say what you mean?
Saying what one means is also called honesty. Being blunt can interfere and offend other people. How about being honest and tactful?

Consider by Paragraph or Seriatim

Three major writers in the field of parliamentary procedure, Robert, Demeter and Keesey, all agree on the proper handling of the motion, "Consider by Paragraph or Seriatim," that each section of a lengthy resolution, or report, be perfected section by section without vote. The Chair of the committee reporting, or the secretary, reads each section. Discussion is held until the Chair is satisfied that no further discussion or amendment is being proposed. At that point, the Chair asks that the next section be read aloud; and that section is treated in the same manner. Likewise all the sections of the resolution or report are considered until all have been perfected.

After all the sections have been perfected, the Chair asks for further amendments. Any section may still be amended, by adding, striking out, or striking out and inserting. After the document has been perfected, a vote is taken to adopt the entire document, probably by the Chair's asking for unanimous approval.

The preamble, if there is one, is considered in the same manner, separate from the consideration of the resolution or report, and after the consideration of the resolution or report.

It may happen that a report or resolution presented to an assembly is acceptable, except for one section. While it may appear expeditious to move to accept all but that one section, it is not expeditious because two fallacious assumptions on the part of the maker of the motion:
a. The other members agree that only the one section is not acceptable, and
b. The other members are satisfied with the package with the voting on all but the one section.

A more prudent approach is to consider the document presented section by section. In the process of so considering, the "controversial" section will come up for consideration. The section is thus not singled out as being controversial, but may receive the same amount of consideration as the other sections.

There is also the added advantage of a methodical approach that is perceived easily by the members of the assembly. For example, if all but "section 5" were to be considered, then there would be some confusion as to which was "section 5," to name just a superficial problem. And the probability of confusion is greater than the anticipated saving of time through adopting the majority of a resolution.

There is a sharp difference between "amending bylaws" and "adopting bylaws." The former requires previous notice and a 2/3 vote for change; the latter requires a simple majority vote, though previous notice is obviously a prudent procedure.

Bylaws are more frequently amended than they are revised, for it is more likely that sections of bylaws will be amended than the whole document revised. It is axiomatic that the preparation for amending of bylaws be carried out with careful preparation of those proposing amendments, and the clear informing of the members of the assembly who must vote on the proposed amendment. It is difficult to prepare too carefully amendments for the consideration of the assembly, since those amendments may well carry emotional as well as legal overtones.

In a series of resolutions, concerning which consideration by the assembly is required, Robert says, "Sometimes a series of independent resolutions relating to completely different subjects is offered by a single main motion . . . where the subjects are independent, any resolution in the series must be taken up and voted on separately at the demand of a single member." Conversely, Robert points out that should the Chair suggest consideration by paragraph, a member may move to have the resolution considered as a whole.

The determination of whether to consider by paragraph or as a whole depends upon the will of the assembly, obviously, predicated upon the nature of the materials being examined. The series of resolutions may be related, but they must not be interlocked - each should stand independently - and should be so written at the time of presentation to the assembly. However, should the resolutions be interlocked, then they must be voted on as a whole, and not separately, for separate vote would not make good sense, nor provide for orderly procedure after the vote.

This writer had an unusual experience recently in an organization that was revising its bylaws. When a motion was made to vote on each section, this writer objected. A friend asked, "Are you sure these sections must be voted on at the end of the consideration of all of them?" The reply was given, "I certainly am." My objection was sustained a short time later when the parliamentarian said, after frantically looking through Robert's, "The vote is taken at the end."

Probably no great harm would have been done had the vote been taken section by section, but harm could have resulted, if a section previously adopted came into conflict with one then being considered. Though no great credit belongs to anyone for knowing the proper procedure, there is no substitute for the self-confidence that springs from knowing, and knowing that one knows. Though consideration by paragraph is somewhat complex, it is logical, and its use requires easy familiarity on the part of the Chair - unless the Chair has an excellent parliamentarian!

Consider by Paragraph or Seriatim - Another View

In long or complicated motions, especially in revision of bylaws, consideration by paragraph or seriatim is usually advisable. The motion allows consideration of the several parts individually, or as a whole. It may happen that only one section of a series of a resolution is controversial. If so, then that one section can be set aside while the others are considered, but not adopted. If all the sections of a resolution are acceptable to the assembly, they can then be adopted with one motion.

There is a very good reason for considering each section individually until all sections are acceptable, until no additional amendments are offered for the sections of the document. After all the sections have been perfected through amendment, all the "whereases" are satisfactory to the assembly, then the revised sections are voted on as a whole.

Notice what happens if each section is adopted by vote of the assembly before going onto the next section. Section 1, being adopted, may come into conflict with Section 3. The assembly is helpless to revise #1 until it has a special meeting for that purpose. One may not say, "Since #3 comes in conflict with #1, let's forget the vote for #1, and adopt #3."

I warned a group of therapists from the Midwest in New York City about the danger of adopting section by section. One determined chairman of the resolutions committee in presenting the committee's recommendations, insisted that each section be voted on as it came up. Fortunately, nothing untoward happened, the several sections were adopted individually, and, as far as I know, the organization has lived happily ever after.

The proper procedure is simple and rigid. The amendments to the bylaws are presented to the assembly as a whole. At this point, two procedures may be followed. The first procedure is to have the chairman of the resolutions committee present them, look at the chair and say, "Madam President, the Resolutions Committee recommends the adoption of all the sections of the resolution." The chair then says, "Are you ready to vote, or are you ready for the question? If there is no objection, the chair will declare them adopted. The chair, seeing no one seeking the floor, declares these bylaws amendments adopted. They become integral and equal parts of the bylaws immediately."

Of course, there could be a time frame introduced, such as "by December 1, 1996," before which specified time the amendments will not become part of the bylaws. But that time proviso should be made **before** the amendments are considered for the time frame may well determine the votes of many of the members of the assembly. Without an adopted time frame, the amendments become parts of the bylaws immediately.

Assuming that the adoption of amendment #5 comes into conflict with amendment #1, the elimination of the conflict should take place as soon as possible. It is understandable that with the multiple revisions to proposed amendments in committee, a conflicting relationship between the two proposed amendments might not show up until the amendments are presented to the assembly. Thus, after all five amendments have been considered (not voted on), all are open to further amendment.

Member Lauryl: Madam President, amendment #1 specifies our meetings shall be held the last Friday of each month. This amendment will give us an irregular pattern of schedule of meetings because some months have five Fridays. I move to strike out the words "last Friday" and insert "fourth Friday."

President Cynthya: The member's point is well taken. To strike out and insert is one motion, thus requires only one vote. We are voting only on Member Lauryl's motion to change within the proposed amendment. Voting on this amendment will take place at the same time all the other amendments are voted on. All in favor of striking out "last Friday" and insert "fourth Friday," vote "aye." Those opposed, vote "no." The amendment to the amendment is adopted. If there is no more discussion or amendments, are you ready for the question, the question being the adoption of all the amendments as they now stand. All In favor . . . .

The preamble to a series of resolutions is adopted last for the obvious reason that amendments to the "whereases" may change the preamble. The "whereases" justify the "Be it resolved," giving supporting reasons for making the resolution. Each "whereas" is perfected - but not voted on; the preamble is perfected - but not voted on. When the document is completed, the chair having said, "There being no one seeking the floor to amend the resolution, the chair declares the document ready for your vote. All in favor . . . ."

The chair may not say, "The adopted amendments to the bylaws will become part of the bylaws on December 1, 1996," unless authorized by the assembly. He may *think* he knows what the assembly wants, but he is not a mind reader, nor does the mythical "power of the chair" allow him to insert a time frame. Should the chair, acting perhaps in good faith, dictate to the assembly what it **needs**, then some hardy soul had better jump up and shout, "I appeal the decision of the chair."

What appealing does is determine that the decision of the chair is the same as the decision of the assembly. Appealing a decision of the chair should not be interpreted as an assault on the authority or dignity of the chair. It does emphasize that the chair serves the needs of the assembly, that he may not unilaterally assert decisions not made by the assembly because he or she thinks that is what the assembly wants. Periodically, some chairmen need to be reminded that the chair is an expediter, a channel for the power of the assembly, not an all-wise czar telling the ignorant plebeians their need implying they are too ignorant to know their own needs.

The obligation of the chair is to explain the appeal procedure. Underlying all parliamentary procedure is the thrust to find and impose the majority will: what aids that aim is good; what thwarts it is bad. If the chair bridles at an appeal to his or her decision, that person should not preside or should learn to preside. It is axiomatic that too frequent appeals to the decisions of the chair can weaken the authority and effectiveness of the chair; but wrong must not prevail simply because of too tender regard of the feelings of the chair, and a consequent insufficient regard for the will of the assembly.

In voting for resolution, a simple majority vote is sufficient for adoption. In the case of amendments to bylaws, probably a two-thirds vote is required, a two-thirds vote being the usual requirement in revision of bylaws in most organizations. The proper vote is that specified in the bylaws.

The steps presented above are rigid, but following them precludes reasonable objections to procedures or adoptions. As the chair, it is better to be considered meticulous, even dull, than to be considered hasty. The suspicion of haste can seriously undermine the effectiveness of the chair. When members have unresolved doubts in meetings, they usually direct their suspicions to the chair. The chair must preside defensively, therefore, explaining and repeating procedures for the dull, the inattentive, and the ornery.

Model for a Resolution

"Whereas, the professional basketball season in this country overlaps the professional baseball season; and
Whereas, baseball is recognized as the major sport of the United States; now, therefore, be it
Resolved, that all professional basketball seasons terminate by April 1st of each year."

There can be variations: many more "whereases," and multiple "Resolutions," and Robert is not the end all of resolution writing; but departure from his format must be taken deliberately, with good reason, if the document is to be presented to the assembly. One must not add to the complexity of getting a resolution adopted the needless complication of argument about its format.

Questions and Answers

1. Why the complicated title, "Consider by paragraph or seriatim?"
One must remember that parliamentary procedure, and its terminology have been developing since the 13th century in England. The term holds on because it still serves a need, and no other term has supplanted it.

2. Isn't your statement extreme that once an amendment is voted on, it cannot be changed, even though a subsequent amendment nullifies it? The people who voted for the amendment in the first place are still present. Why can't they just revote?
There must be a termination point. Otherwise, all decisions would be impermanent, and no one would have the confidence of closure. A revote may take place only if there is widespread confusion about what was voted on, or fraud has been committed.

3. Isn't this procedure very complicated?
It certainly can be. It ranks with Amend Something Previously Adopted, separating double motions, and substitution motions in its complexity. Still, it has its use and needs to be in the lexicon of every presider.

CHAPTER XI - Reconsideration
"To Reconsider" strategy after close vote loss

Parliamentary procedure came to us Americans through the British parliamentary system with one distinctive American addition - reconsideration. Reconsideration means precisely what it says, that is, to reconsider a past action of the assembly, possibly because new information has been secured that makes the passage of the previous motion impractical, illegal, or even dangerous.

In the summer of 1941, six months before the Pearl Harbor attack, the Congress was debating the extension of the unpopular Selective Service Act due to expire in October, 1941. One popular saying at the time was OHIO, Over the Hill in October, a threat to desert at the expiration of the original act. Accompanying the distaste for compulsory military service was the widespread belief that World War 11 was a foreign war, alien to American interests. George Washington was quoted a great deal, especially his exhortation, "Avoid foreign entanglements."

The proponents of the draft extension authorization were dismayed by the vote in the House of Representatives that defeated the extension of the draft. So proponents of draft extension scurried among the House members, had the bill reconsidered, and passed it by one vote! Had the draft not been extended, America would have entered World War 11 with only a small volunteer army.

Reconsider simply means to consider a previous vote taken by the assembly within twenty-four hours. Passage of the motion to reconsider brings the previous question again before the assembly as if the motion had not been voted on previously. Passage of the motion to reconsider does not change the original vote it simply brings the opportunity for debate and possible amendment of the original motion to members of the assembly, and a chance to vote again.

One controversial requirement of reconsideration is that any member moving reconsideration must have voted with the prevailing side at the original vote. That is, if the original was passed, only a member voting for passage is permitted to move for reconsideration. There are sharp differences among parliamentarians about the restriction of having voted with the prevailing side as a prerequisite to moving to reconsider. Robert states clearly, "It can be made only by a member who voted with the prevailing side" (p. 265).

Alice Sturgis paraphrases Luther Cushing, "eminent lawyer and parliamentarian," who wrote in his manual of 1844 that reconsider can be made by any member, just as any member can make any other motion. She opposes the restriction of moving to reconsider to those who voted with the prevailing side and adds, ". . . any member has the right to propose any motion, regardless of how he voted previously, unless the organization adopts a rule limiting this right." Reconsider simply means to consider a previous vote taken by the assembly, within twenty-four hours. (p. 41)

Demeter agrees with Robert, stipulating "Reconsideration in the main body . . . can be moved only by one who voted on the prevailing side of the motion."

An argument for the Robert/ Demeter position can easily be exemplified:

Joel Lane moved for reconsideration of a motion he had voted against, the vote on the motion being 18 for, 2 against. The assembly had clearly voted its support for the motion, yet Joel, according to Alice Sturgis, has the right to move for reconsideration.

Theoretically, every motion any member voted against could be called up for reconsideration, thus extending the time of the meeting, and requiring members to consider what they had clearly approved. It must be pointed out that the vote for reconsideration by the two persons who voted against the motion will hardly prove persuasive to the eighteen people who just voted for it. Before the two members who voted against the adopted motion bring it up, they must provide additional information that will prove persuasive to the majority who voted for the motion.

The pivotal question is: should a defeated minority have the parliamentary right to bring a defeated motion again before the assembly solely because they are members? Or should they not have this right because the assembly has already voted for the motion, and should not be forced to consider the adopted motion again? Should the two-vote minority tail wag the eighteen-vote majority dog?

Ray Keesey, our fourth prominent parliamentarian, holds with Alice Sturgis, writing, "The motion To Reconsider may be made by any member, and may be applied to affirmative or negative votes on main motions, but not to votes or motions . . . which have already resulted in irreversible action" (p.76).

The "infrequently used motion to reconsider" (Keesey P. 76) is designed to reverse ill-advised actions by the assembly. For example, if a non-profit-making organization endorses a political candidate, it risks losing its tax-exempt status. The information about the possible jeopardy resulting from the endorsement of a political candidate will undoubtedly cause the assembly to reverse its previous action. As to the limitation that only a member voting with the prevailing side can introduce this motion to reconsider, the limitation can be overcome by a member who voted with the losing side asking a member voting for the prevailing side to move to reconsider. The information would surely be persuasive and cause the prevailing side member to move to reconsider.

To Reconsider belongs to that small group of six motions that bring a question again before the assembly, Class B. It does require a second, does not allow debate or amendment, and is passed by a majority vote. A motion to reconsider cannot itself be reconsidered.

A personal note - parliamentarians memorize much material, they need devices, such as mnemonics, or acronyms, to help. This unusual motion carries the memory aid of BSMD, the words, Bill Southworth Mule Driver. By nature a memory aid should be ridiculous to be valuable; but when a parliamentarian is sitting at a convention, with two hundred members of the assembly looking at him and is asked, "How do we go about reconsidering this motion," that silly phrase allows the parliamentarian to write down BSMD quickly, and then respond confidently and accurately.

There is a rule of thumb that the motion To Reconsider must be made within twenty-four hours of the passage of the adopted motion to be considered. Neither Rescind nor Amend Something Previously Adopted has the restrictive time element of To Reconsider.

Some Considerations of Reconsideration

Knowledgeable parliamentarians recognize that reconsider is a uniquely American parliamentary procedure, that it is not used by the British from whom we inherited our system of parliamentary procedure. Its status in America is verified by its universal acceptance among American authorities even the iconoclastic Mr. Keesey.

One interesting variation on reconsider is offered by Alice Sturgis. While the other authorities agree that the person moving to reconsider in an assembly must have voted on the prevailing side, Alice Sturgis insists that any member may move to reconsider. She buttresses her position by pointing out that the courts have ruled that any member may propose a motion, not excluding the motion to reconsider. Let us consider a concrete example:

> A main motion was adopted by the assembly, 20 to 3. Generally, reconsideration would not be proposed because the majority would be required to negate its vote, reverse itself to reconsider a motion that it has just passed overwhelmingly. Unless new and convincing information were given to the majority, it is difficult to imagine circumstances under which the majority would reconsider.
>
> If the three members on the losing side were to move for reconsideration, they would be asking the assembly to consider anew a motion it had already passed. The question arises - Is the minority maneuvering the majority through a parliamentary ploy?

An even wider implication is that the losing side, not being able to persuade the majority during the debate on the motion, is trying to undo what the majority has decided-in effect, putting the adopted motion under double jeopardy. Logically, without additional persuasive information, the losing side cannot even expect a reconsideration of the vote, let alone another opportunity to defeat the motion. Further, if every adopted motion is subject to reconsideration, the members can never feel sure that any motion adopted by the majority is final. By allowing reconsideration to be introduced by any three minority members as a right, much mischief can be caused by determined people and the time wasted by the organization through the machinations of these willful people can be enormous.

One counter argument for allowing minority members to move to reconsider is the chair's right to rule the motion frivolous. But if the members have the right to move to reconsider, is it prudent for the chair to rule out the motion? But here confusion is compounded. Not only must the body consider a motion to reconsider made by a person who voted in the minority, it can now become involved in overruling the chair if the motion of the two members to reconsider is denied by the chair. Challenge of the chair should be made charily - not for the preservation of the pride of the presider, but for the preservation of the prestige and position of the chair, whoever is presiding.

The minority can cynically exploit its opportunities to delay and possibly defeat the will of the majority, if determined to have its way - at whatever cost. The obligation of all members to support the position taken by the assembly, even though some disagreed, is reasonable and is widely ignored. The power of the vote of the individual member is augmented by the votes of the other members.

The member who disagrees with the majority rule cannot seize the best of two worlds when he agrees with the majority, he supports the organization's position; when he disagrees, he refuses to accept the organization's position. Once a decision of an organization is made, it is incumbent on *all* members to support that decision *until* such time as the dissenting member can convince a majority of the members that the organization's position is wrong,

The emphasis must be on the will of the majority of the group - the organization itself. Demanding reconsideration simply because one is allowed to so demand erodes the basis of organization, over-emphasizing the right of the member to the detriment of the other members and of the organization.

There is general support for reconsideration among parliamentary authorities. The problem concerning it is: by whom may it be used? While there is judicial opinion that all may use it, the basis for the Sturgis position, a stronger case can be made for restricting the use of the motion to members who voted with the prevailing side. It continues to be true that the rights of the minority must be protected; but not at the expense of the rights of the majority, for by eroding the rights of the majority, the basis of majority rule is eroded; and majority rule is the basis of democratic assemblies.

Reconsider and Enter on the Minutes

One legitimate criticism of parliamentary procedure is its use of complex and archaic language:
"I call for the previous question" really means "I ask for a vote on the *pending* question."
"Call for the orders of the day" means "Stick to the agenda."
"Lay on the table" means "Set it aside until other substantial business has been accomplished."
"Division of the assembly" means "Take a standing vote."
"Suspend the rules" means "Change the agenda because of extraordinary circumstances."
"Take from the table" means "Consider now what was put aside previously."
But the oddest ball of all is "Reconsider and enter on the minutes."

"Reconsider" is clear enough. Robert holds that only a person who voted with the prevailing side may move to reconsider, while Sturgis (p. 41) quoting Cushing, 19th Century parliamentarian, insists that every member has the right to move to reconsider. Whatever the bases for reconsideration, its meaning is easily understood: "that the question shall come before the assembly again as if it had not previously been considered" (Robert, p. 77).

"Enter on the minutes" means two members may so move with the result that the motion on the floor is suspended and cannot be considered further at that time. All actions on the motion cease immediately.

The purpose of reconsider and enter on the minutes, as explained by Robert (pp 326-8), is to prevent an unrepresentative quorum from adopting a motion that would have been rejected were the quorum representative of the membership. For example, at the end of a long meeting, many members had left the hall, but a quorum remains. A motion is made and passed to redecorate the clubhouse. Prudence Pepper, a knowledgeable member, anticipating adoption of this motion she opposes, votes to adopt, knowing that having voted on the prevailing side she will be able to move to reconsider later.

Prudence goes out to the bar and gets her supporting fellow members, then comes back into the hall. Prudence knows she can wait no longer than to the next day before her motion is outlawed by time. Immediately, Prudence persuades Harker Haines to second the motion. Harker cooperates, and all consideration of the motion stops; no discussion.

Some parliamentary authorities, Keesey particularly, objects to "Reconsider and enter on the minutes," responding at length (pp 91-92), "It is difficult to understand how a motion whose purpose is to prevent the rule of the majority from prevailing can be defended. Its use permits the minority to determine what constitutes valid action on the part of the majority. This contradicts a basic principle of parliamentary law, that of majority rule." Other authorities point out that two people can thwart the will of a large assembly for 24 hours by using this parliamentary procedure. Majority rule is scorned when two members can frustrate the will of a hundred members by using this little-known procedure.

One other objection is the presumption of Prudence and Harker that they alone know the will of the membership of this club. While they may suspect that the larger number of members will disallow the motion to redecorate the clubhouse, they are speculating; and while they are trying to confirm their speculation by button-holing other members, the majority decision to redecorate the clubhouse is held up for twenty-four hours.

Robert (p. 329) points out the danger of overuse of the motion by a willful minority to prevent action taken by the members. If, for instance, two members misuse the motion by moving to reconsider and enter on the minutes a vote which requires action before the next regular meeting then they circumvent the will of the other members. (Robert, p. 329) Robert further opines that the adoption of an adjourned meeting time may well cause the withdrawal of the motion to reconsider and enter on the minutes. The majority will of the members will be determined at the adjourned meeting.

There is in "Reconsider and enter on the minutes" an uneasy use of procedure to negate a properly adopted motion, opposed by only two people. Two prescient, dedicated members may by the use of this motion prevent a costly mistake; but the assumption that wisdom resides only in Prudence Pepper and Harker Haines smacks too much of egocentric infallibility, and imputes docility at best to the majority, or stupidity at the worst. To balance the picture somewhat, at the next meeting any one member may call up the motion to reconsider at an appropriate time. While reconsider and enter on the minutes requires two members to enact, bringing up the delayed motion requires only one member.

CHAPTER XII - The Parliamentarian
Duties of the Parliamentarian

Presiders who avoid the services of parliamentarians do so for wrong reasons. The presiders fear:
1. The parliamentarian will embarrass them by openly requiring the presiders to follow the bylaws of the organization and the rules of Robert.
2. Any decision made by the chair may be overturned by the parliamentarian, acting as appeal judge.
3. The parliamentarian will take over and control the meeting.
4. The parliamentarian will function as schoolmaster/top sergeant/stern parent.

Parliamentary authorities describe the role of the parliamentarian. Demeter says, "He is appointed primarily to advise the presiding officer on questions of parliamentary law and procedure, thus helping to safeguard the rights and privileges of all the members equally, and to help transact the business of the assembly legally and efficiently. The parliamentarian should be strictly non-partisan at all times" (p.253). Keesey adds: "In case of extreme inability to conduct a meeting, the presiding officer may rely heavily on the parliamentarian, even to the extent of having him preside temporarily" (p. 98).

While it is better for the parliamentarian not to be a member of the organization, it is legitimate for him to be a member and still be parliamentarian. However, he must become involved in deliberations charily and vote unobstructively, for he must protect his nonpartisan status. As a rule, he should vote in all secret ballots, but avoid *viva voce* and standing votes.

Alice Sturgis comments, "The more a presiding officer knows about parliamentary law, the more he appreciates the fact that a parliamentarian can relieve him of responsibility for procedural problems and details so that the presiding officer is free to concentrate on reactions and concerns of the members and on the over-all progress and tone of the meeting. Then he can proceed with confidence and poise" (p.231).

Primary emphasis must be placed on the central role of the parliamentarian: Counsel to the chair. Ideally, the parliamentarian confines his activities to aiding the chair in procedural matters. He writes notes, talks quietly with the presider, and helps in keeping tabs on who speaks at which microphone next, for example, and totaling the ballot numbers provided by the tellers.

The parliamentarian must eschew the mantle of infallibility for two important reasons: an attitude of his showing his disapproval of actions taken by the presider can quickly spoil the rapport between presider and parliamentarian. Second, the presider knows more about the organization than the parliamentarian does. The parliamentarian proposes, the presider disposes. As the presider has no obligation to follow the advice and counsel of the parliamentarian, so the parliamentarian has no responsibility for the actions of the presider.

The picture of the presider/parliamentarian team is clear: the presider is concerned primarily with substance, the parliamentarian primarily with procedure. One parliamentarian, after being introduced in a highly charged meeting, said "My concern is procedure. I don't care if you paint this condominium purple, because I have no financial interest in it or fiduciary responsibility for it. My purpose is to help you decide what you want to do in an orderly and democratic manner." Thereafter, he was accepted by the condo unit owners.

The bishop at one convention made a decision. The member standing challenged the chair, asking, "What does the parliamentarian think?" Of course, the parliamentarian wisely refused to answer. When pressed he replied, "You elected the bishop to preside. I am not a court of appeal. My status is advisor to the chair. I speak only when and if asked by the chair to speak." Then, tactfully, "If you want an opinion on a problem, you may speak to me when I am free, and I'll be happy to talk with you."

The selection of the parliamentarian for a convention, for instance, follows a narrow pattern: by the chair with the prior or later consent of the executive board; by the body itself; by the executive board; or as provided in the bylaws (Demeter, p. 263). Central to any choice of parliamentarian is the confident working relationship between the presider and the parliamentarian. The parliamentarian recognizes his subordinate role, and enjoys it; and if he cannot, he should remove himself.

Preferably, the parliamentarian is retained weeks before the actual convention. He requires a set of bylaws and other pertinent data, such as minutes of a previous convention for study and greater understanding of the organization to be served. Before the convention begins, the parliamentarian must have a half-hour with the presider so that lines of understanding can develop, and a working relationship initiated.

The presider will preside, the parliamentarian will work cooperatively with the chair toward the common goal of presider, assembly, and parliamentarian: The expeditious and democratic handling of the business of the assembly. Whatever honorable means the parliamentarian can use to gain that common end must be used by him. If that involves timing speakers, keeping track of lines at microphones, working with the secretary, so be it. The parliamentarian must not take himself too seriously by remembering Chesterton's axiom, "I don't take myself seriously, but I take my ideas seriously."

It is ironic that by submerging his procedural preferences to the decision of the chair, the parliamentarian solidifies his position as a genuine contributor to the convention. His skill is hired, not his wishes; and he engenders respect by confining himself within the narrow confines of the parliamentarian's role. Participants generally respect what they understand; and if they understand the primary role of the parliamentarian, and the parliamentarian also respects that role by restricting himself it, he enjoys the assembly's appreciation. And, what is most important, the convention's business is handled well.

After the convention is over, what remains is what was accomplished, not how it was accomplished. And if the parliamentarian has contributed to the success of a convention, he will enjoy personal and professional satisfaction that beggars the annoyance of being overruled occasionally by the chair.

Q. In our club, all the nominations are seconded. Are we following Robert's Rules?
A. No, but the matter has no significance. Robert states that it is not required to second nominations. However, if your club has been seconding nominations and wants to continue to second them, there should be no barrier put in the way of continuing a practice that is generally harmless. It can be argued that this practice can embarrass a person whose nomination is not seconded; but, if the person cannot get a second, the person probably cannot win an election. Also, nominations should be made by placing in nomination the name of any qualified person spoken aloud.

Q. What about putting the name of each seconder in the minutes?

A. Not a good idea. It gives a certain stature to members whose only contribution is to say a word aloud that does not commit them to support or oppose a motion. All a seconder does by seconding is insure the motion is placed before the assembly.

Q. Must a person who makes a motion support that motion?
A. No, because the discussion that follows the placing of his motion before the house may cause the person to change his mind, and oppose the motion he made. However, the person making a motion may not talk against that motion.

Q. After a committee has made its recommendations to the assembly, may a member of that committee speak against the recommendations of the committee of which he was a part?
A. Yes. Once the committee recommendations have been presented to the assembly, every member has a right to join in the debate. Functionally, once the committee recommendations have been made, the committee no longer exists. Actually, the committee continues to exist until the assembly has acted on its recommendations. Thereafter, the committee no longer exists.

Q. When are the recommendations of committee seconded?
A. When the committee is a committee of one. Otherwise, the recommendations of the committee are seconded by the positive vote of the committee before they are presented to the assembly.

The Parliamentarian and the Olympic Committee

When I received an unexpected telephone call in December, 1983 from an of official of the Executive Committee of the Olympic Committee, asking me to serve as parliamentarian for a meeting to be held in New York City, I quickly agreed. Serving the Olympic Committee would be prestigious, and I looked forward to a reasonable fee for my services.

At the time I was asked, I was serving the National Association of Parliamentarians as district director for New York and the New England states. Thus, my name was prominent and I fulfilled the requirement of the constitution of the Olympic Committee to have a registered parliamentarian for each executive board meeting. Parenthetically, I learned that former meetings had run two and three days, that such lengthy meetings were financially burdensome to some of the members of the committee. and that shortening the meetings - through better organization of the meetings - was vital to the welfare of the Committee. I asked for the usual documents: the constitution, the bylaws, minutes of a former meeting, and any other pertinent documents.

The bylaws and the constitution were forthcoming and accentuated the advantage of having bylaws solely, for in the two documents identical subjects were treated differently. Two adversaries could quote basic documents to prove their points - and each would be right! The resulting confusion could cause bad feelings; and the defense that the constitution is senior in stature to the bylaws is untenable.

I suspected my status when I was put at the end of the table, as far from the presider as I could be without falling off the dais. A parliamentarian was required by the constitution, but was not considered functionally necessary. That feeling of not being necessary was emphasized when I introduced myself to William Simon, former Secretary of the Treasury, president of the Olympic Committee.

I said, "Good morning, Mr. Simon. I'm your parliamentarian."

"Oh, I don't need any help," he said in a booming voice. "I've been doing this for twenty years."

Actually, his assessment was largely accurate. He presided with knowledge and tact. Only the presentation of four recommendations from a committee, one of which was not ready for presentation, caused a conference between the chairman and me. It is ironic that I received praise for my counsel from two members at the head table - and in a matter so simple!

Most of the time I sat next to a retired lieutenant general. We talked about general officers of the Marine Corps of World War II vintage. Otherwise, I followed the flow of the meeting conscientiously, though I was superfluous in the eyes of the chair.

Only one matter came up that caused me to walk to the presider - not Mr. Simon - and that was the adoption of a motion, followed by the adoption of another motion that directly contradicted the first motion. The presider brushed me off courteously, but let the contradiction stand, assuming that participants would simply forget the first motion and remember the second.

****

A completely different experience happened when I served my first convention of the Licensed Practical Nurses and Allied Health Services Union in the Thousand Islands of New York State. I was asked to serve because of the perceived politicizing of a former parliamentarian in the substantive decisions of the organization. So a previous parliamentarian was contacted, who in turn contacted

Tom Germano, director of the Labor Institute of Cornell University at Farmingdale College. I served in the parliamentarian role and all went well then, and for five years of subsequent service.

"To serve, not to be served' is an honored phrase, particularly applicable to parliamentarians. If parliamentarians seek and use additional ways to serve, they have the satisfaction of doing more than is required; and the recipients of that additional service will respond with a stipend and gratitude, thus providing the parliamentarian a double return from serving well.

****

I did all the right things: I had sought and studied the pertinent documents, developed a rapport with the presider, and was ready to sit next to the presider, the bishop. It was my first Lutheran convention - in fact, it was my first convention of any kind! I was almost blissful in my self-confidence, self-confidence that was bolstered by the skill and experience of the presiding bishop.

The first convention day, Saturday, went so well a friend called me a lousy parliamentarian. I countered with, "I am a very good parliamentarian. Look how smoothly the meeting is going." That was Saturday!

On Sunday, about 11 A.M., I had happily confirmed the bishop's decision to disallow the introduction of a second motion when there was already a motion on the floor. To confirm my knowledge, I looked up the applicable passage, and was happily congratulating myself on my knowledge when I became aware that the assembly was perfectly quiet, and the bishop was looking at me with his big brown inquisitive eyes, obviously expecting me to respond to some question about which I had not the slightest inkling. Covering my confusion as best I could, I walked over to the bishop, asked the bishop to repeat the question, and was relieved to find it was an easy question.

After the convention was over, the bishop generously evaluated my service to him, comparing me favorably with parliamentarians he had known in the past, ranging from good to ". . . flustered, disruptive, pompous, and overbearing." I was understandably lucky being compared with less-than-adequate ''parliamentarians'.'' First convention - satisfied bishop - satisfied assembly. Altogether I served the bishop in five conventions - and we are still friends.

****

A group of health care professionals retained my services as parliamentarian for their annual convention in New York City. They were a pleasant group, and listened to my advice and counsel - except for the chairman of the constitution committee.

She was ready to present five constitutional amendments. I suggested that she introduce the amendments separately, which she agreed to. I suggested that all be discussed, but that none be voted on until all had been discussed. I was following the direction of Robert, who points out that the adoption of one amendment may conflict with subsequent amendments, and that the resulting conflict among the amendments could not be resolved until another convention.

She persisted. Not only did she present the amendments singly, and take a vote on each, she announced the results of the voting! Was she wrong? Procedurally, she was wrong; functionally, the convention delegates agreed with her.

That incident again reminded me that the role of the parliamentarian is to advise, and counsel - nothing more. An assembly may do what it wants, so long as it does not come into conflict with the law or its own bylaws. However, if the assembly wants to come in conflict with the law or its own constitution, it does so at its own peril. The parliamentarian shares no responsibility for the decisions of the assembly.

The Parliamentarian and the Tellers

The parliamentarian is the team leader of the tellers. He organizes them, directs them, instructs them - and they report to him. At least one half-hour before the beginning of a convention, the parliamentarian meets with the tellers, perhaps twelve volunteer workers in a convention of 200 delegates.

At the first meeting, the parliamentarian, with the cooperation of the chair, forms two teams, A & B, C & D. The A & B team count the votes in the left half of the hall, the C & D team the right half of the hall. A faces B as the two count the votes in the left half of the hall, compare their individual numbers at the end of the fifth row. A tells the delegates when to lower their voting cards. At the back of the section if A and B agree on the total, B takes the total of the positive votes to the parliamentarian, who tabulates the votes with the secretary.

Likewise, the C & D team, counting the ten tables on the right side of the hall, meet at the back of the section. and compare their individual numbers, C tells the delegates when to lower their voting cards. If they do not agree, a new count is taken, starting from the front of the section. If they agree, D takes the number of votes to the parliamentarian and the secretary.

The parliamentarian and the secretary add up the votes, and agree on the total.

Then, the two teams repeat the count for negative votes, and again compare votes at the back of the two sections. If the two teams of A & B and C & D agree, B and D take the totals to the parliamentarian.

The parliamentarian and the secretary form another team whose purpose is to agree on the total number of votes, and to provide that total to the chair. The *chair* announces the results of the voting.

The above prescription is rigid but necessary. In dealing with situations with many people present, there must be the confidence that the delegates understand what they are voting on. If casualness prevails, bewilderment will result that will eventually have to be corrected by rigid procedures.

Some presiders wait until there is a need for a standing counted vote, and then appoint tellers. This dereliction of the presider is indefensible: If there is a perceived need for voting, there is need to provide for standing, counted voting. If there is standing counted voting, there is a need for tellers. And tellers must be instructed as a group before they start to work to avoid the confusion that results from jerrybuilding the process of counting only when its use is urgent and immediate.

The chair must announce the result of the vote. The announcement of the vote by the secretary, for instance, functionally diminishes the status of the chair and disproportionately enlarges the role of the secretary.

The tellers have one more important function - the counting of the ballots. A prescription:
1. Set up a separate room for the tellers.
2. Set up two teams of three persons each. These two teams will tabulate the vote, one person counting aloud, the other person tabulating by writing the spoken number on the appropriate ballot. For example, when A says "1," B writes "1" on the first ballot. When A says "2," B writes "2" on the second ballot. The remaining ballots are counted aloud and recorded in the same manner. The third member of the team checks to see that the ballots are being counted and recorded accurately.

3. The two teams take their results to the parliamentarian and the secretary who check the totals of each team before giving the grand total to the chair.

4. The two teams of tellers are thanked and asked to stand by for further duties.

A plan must be developed for each situation potentially requiring a standing, counted vote. Setting up an arrangement for tabulating votes must be done deliberately before it is needed. It may prove unnecessary; but so is a fire department until there is a fire.

One final thought: Get the cooperation of the presider before you set up a tellers' arrangement. There is nothing more deflating than to work with a chair so inexperienced that it thinks the tellers unnecessary until there is obvious need for them, or fussily interferes with the tellers and the parliamentarian.

Using hindsight, it was obviously necessary to be ready for tellers to tabulate a counted vote. The wise chair provides for contingencies before they happen. The good parliamentarian thinks in such provident terms, and presses hard for them before the meeting. If the chair does not cooperate, the parliamentarian helps the chair to unravel the discord generated by the chair's failure.

Counting Ballots In A Convention

This chart illustrates the above article

A & B
xxxxxxxxx
xxxxxxxxx
xxxxxxxxx
xxxxxxxxx
xxxxxxxxx
xxxxxxxxx
xxxxxxxxx
xxxxxxxxx
xxxxxxxxx
Sec. Parl.
C & D
xxxxxxxxx
xxxxxxxxx
xxxxxxxxx
xxxxxxxxx
xxxxxxxxx
xxxxxxxxx
xxxxxxxxx
xxxxxxxxx
xxxxxxxxx
Presider

Key - Green Cards "yes," Red Cards "no"

1. Team **A & B** count the same cards. A tells the delegates when to lower their cards. B takes the agreed upon tally to the secretary/ parliamentarian. A & B compare and agree on the count at the back of their section.

2. Team **C&D** count the same (cards) and agree on the count at the back of section. **C** tells the delegates when to lower their cards. **D** takes the agreed upon tally to the secretary/ parliamentarian.

3. The secretary/parliamentarian total the numbers from teams **A&B, C&D,** agree upon the totals, and give the totals to the chair.

4. The *chair* announces the results of the vote.

The Parliamentarian and the IRS

Closely connected with the revenue that the active parliamentarian can develop is the handling of that money, especially the reporting of it to the IRS. While what follows must necessarily be in general terms because every parliamentarian has a different report to make, it is hoped that generalization can be developed from those particulars.

Careful records have been kept of all my parliamentary activities: letters written to potential clients; letters written to former clients; meetings attended; work done; and expenses incurred, especially expenses incurred. If a parliamentarian must travel to fulfill his obligation to sit as a parliamentarian, then mileage records should be kept, and entered as expenses of a paid parliamentarian.

The expense of office supplies can become significant if one is active in giving parliamentary opinions. While one is required to be accurate in accounting for expenses incurred one must not think of the IRS as some monster just waiting to catch the expense item that is not incontrovertibly provable.

The costs of membership are deductible items. Specifically, dues are deductible, as are non-reimbursed expenses incurred as a concommitant of being a member of an established not-for-profit organization. Suppose that you meet with other parliamentarians to serve the specific needs of the organization, then certainly you should consider listing that expense as a deductible item. I was told recently that one may not deduct one's usual fee for the contribution of services. Specifically, I thought that I could deduct my usual fee for serving as the bishop's parliamentarian without charge. I was told that I could only take expenses for the free service rendered!

There should be a reasonable attitude toward the IRS: one should not expect to deduct more than is allowed; but one should deduct what is allowed, and do so confidently. Alas! Our income tax system is so complicated that I find it necessary to hire a tax person to help with my income tax return. I am confident that having that person's help has saved me far more than the fee for preparing my income tax return. I simply give him the information and let him fill out the form, relying upon his knowledge about reasonable deductions in connection with a business.

There is sometimes a fear that one should not report to the IRS unless one makes money every year. While income from parliamentary procedure may vary from year to year, once you start reporting you should not be deterred by a lean year. To buttress your position further, you should consider setting up a business, registered with your local political unit.

Let me be specific. I registered with the Suffolk County Clerk's office as a business, simply using: "William Dixon Southworth, Ph.D., Parliamentarian." I soon got mailings asking me to buy office equipment, which made me smile, for I was a small one-man operation. My purpose for filing was twofold: by establishing myself as a business I buttressed my position in claiming part of my residence as necessary for my business, thus allowing a percentage deduction of household costs; and being a business can reassure possible clients of the seriousness of the parliamentarian as a provider of services, rather than someone who is casually concerned with picking up parliamentary work here and there.

It may be that your participation as a parliamentarian does not warrant such involvement with the IRS. In that case, ignore all of the above. It may also be that you enjoy participating in parliamentary activities that could be deductible, but you prefer just to serve without considering the expenses involved. In that case, do not read the above. It may be that you fear even putting down on your income tax that you have made money as a parliamentarian. In that case, ignore all of the above. However, if you have been smoldering because businessmen take clients to lunch and deduct the cost of the lunches for all because business was at least mentioned, perhaps you should consider lawful deductions under the IRS code.

Uncle Sam really wants to play fair with you. He wants you to have your lawful deductions. Honestly and straightforwardly asking for those deductions can result in nothing worse than a non-allowance of those deductions. On the other hand, you might save a little tax money by making provable deductions of expenses connected with your work as a parliamentarian.

The Parliamentarian as Expert Witness

It was a Friday afternoon in April when I received a telephone call from a large labor union business manager in New York City. "We need a parliamentarian. We called Washington and got your name. Are you a parliamentarian?"

"Yes, I am; but who gave you my name in Washington?"

"I don't know. But we have a problem and need your help. Can you meet with us tomorrow at 2:00 p.m. at our headquarters, and then go to Federal Court in Foley Square on Monday at 10:00 a.m.? I don't want to discuss the problem on the phone. We can do that Saturday afternoon. Okay?"

I agreed. On Saturday, I went to a large, affluent labor union headquarters in Manhattan for the conference. The problem was this:

An opposition group to the incumbent executive board was bringing suit in Federal Court, claiming that a motion made by the opposition in a meeting of the union had been miscounted, that the vote taken on the motion carried, and was not defeated as the union leadership claimed.

The lawyer for the union leadership then opened his copy of Robert's to a ten-word phrase in the early part of the book, and asked me, "What does that mean?"

I responded as one should not reply to a lawyer, "I don't know." I should have stalled, saying, "Let me study it."

Thereafter, he took the attitude that he could successfully ignore professional opinion.

Next, a poorly prepared audiovisual cassette was presented, showing the questionable vote. The film showed:
1. A too-small room, with members standing against two walls of the auditorium, others standing and milling around the stage in front of the lectern.
2. The opposition leader moved that his five amendments be handled first.
3. The president stated, "You may ask questions about the motion, but you can't discuss it."
4. After some desultory and unproductive movement on the stage, the opposition leader asked, "What about my motion?"
5. The president took a standing uncounted vote, and declared the motion lost.

On Monday at 9:00 a.m., the executive group, the attorney, and I met at union headquarters, talked generally, and then rode to the Federal Courthouse in Foley Square.

Inside the courtroom, the judge greeted both sides of the disagreement with, "The last time you came in here it was an argument over the distribution of turkeys."

The testimony centered on the interpretation of the standing vote. Three witnesses for the opposition side said they looked around while the vote was taken, and thought the motion passed.

The testimony from the executive group said the motion was defeated.

There were huddles that took place during breaks in the court action. During one of those huddles I told the lawyer for the executive group, "I must confer with you."

"Sure," he said. "But I don't want to put you on the stand because the other attorney will make a fool of you."

"Like hell he will!" I replied. "I know what I'm talking about."

But he would not talk further with me except on one occasion. That occasion was prompted by my having spoken to a man on crutches who had testified for the opposition. The lawyer for the executive group, in a friendly and avuncular way, told me I should not have spoken with the man, and then told me that the law is cold and unfeeling, but that was the way it works.

I felt I was my own man, that the union leadership did not own me, and so long as I was not discussing the case, I could talk with whomever I please. But it was clear the lawyer had learned the mean narrow rules of the courtroom, and clearly revealed his distrust of a non-lawyer's discretion in talking with someone else by arbitrarily dictating that he, the lawyer, would determine with whom I might talk. Still, he would not discuss the role that I could play in resolving the problem.

I came to the conclusion that he did not want to solve the problem definitively after he and the opposing attorney, conferring privately, arrived at an absurd solution: The negative vote on each of the proposed amendments would be taken first. If there was substantial opposition, then the positive vote would be taken. The judge, anxious to clear the case up by 5:00 P.M., and outspokenly eager to have the two attorneys resolve the differences of the case, accepted the solution.

We did not get out of the courthouse by 5:00 P.M. but the case was "resolved" that day. I say "resolved" because the "solution" concocted by two attorneys did not provide for a counted vote, even in their bizarre scheme to count the negative vote first. And who would determine that the negative vote was "close," thus requiring a positive vote?

I drew two obvious conclusions. The attorney for the executive group of the union did not want to defile the sacred soil of attorney turf by conferring with someone whose expertise even slightly, abuts the law. And secondly, by setting up this Rube Goldberg parliamentary contraption, he had sown the seeds for future controversy that could require a return to court for future controversies that could easily have been precluded, but would prove profitable to him.

I left the fetid air of the courtroom for the fresh air of the university campus where the search for truth and personal development happily supplanted the adversarial-minded self-seeking of lawyers in a courtroom.

I was reminded of what Mr. Bumble said in Dickens' Pickwick Papers, " . . . the law is a ass."

What also came to me was my oversight in not detecting that the standing of the opposition leader and a number of other people during the standing vote for, and the standing vote against, the motion rendered the vote for the motion invalid. In effect, those standing during both votes voted twice, thus hopelessly adulterating the vote.

Also, the refusal of the chair to allow discussion of a main motion presented to the union membership was arbitrary and contrary to good parliamentary procedure. However, had a standing counted vote been taken, the vote for and against the motion would have been known, and the need for the court case avoided.

CHAPTER XIII - Membership

Most people belong to organizations that provide one type of membership: Equal membership for all the members. Examples abound: church membership, garden club membership, veterans' organizations, and the PTA. But other kinds of memberships cause confusion.

Ex officio membership, meaning "by virtue of office" is most easily explained by Robert's example (p.473). The governor of a state holds ex officio membership on many boards, all of which he could not possibly attend on a regular basis. While attending such meetings, he has all the rights of the other members, being allowed to make motions, debate, amend, and vote. However, there is a distinction between two types of ex officio members.

The governor should not be counted to determine a quorum since he not a regular member of the committee. There is good reason for not including the governor in the quorum count (Robert, p. 474).

Should an ex officio member of the board also be a member of the organization he has the same obligations as other members. For example, a member may serve as ex officio treasurer of the board because the bylaws of the organization require that only a person properly trained and experienced may serve as treasurer. Thus, the ex officio treasurer has obligations as treasurer and obligations as do other members to serve the organization.

"When an ex officio member of a board ceases to hold the office that entitles him to such membership, his membership on the board terminates automatically." (Robert, p 474). In short, when the governor is no longer governor, he loses his ex officio status on boards authorizing the governor to be an ex officio member.

Too often ex officio membership and honorary membership are confused. While ex officio membership permits full participation, honorary membership is limited to the specifications of the bylaws. Honorary membership may be conferred upon an individual who has served an organization in an outstanding way that merits special recognition. A person who has served the organization for a number of years may be granted honorary membership as an officer or as a member. There are specific universal restrictions on honorary membership.

The honorary member may attend meetings and speak, but may neither make motions nor vote. The payment of dues may be waived for the honorary member; or he may be required to pay them. But it does seem anomalous to grant a long-serving member honorary membership, deny the right to make motions or vote in meetings, and then charge dues. And requiring the honorary member to pay only reduced dues does not offset the basic incongruity of requiring an honorary member to pay dues in an organization that has favored him with honorary membership.

Junior membership, with restricted rights, is frequently granted to otherwise qualified persons who are too young to be full-fledged members. Age eighteen years seems a reasonable requirement for full membership, matching as it does full citizenship that permits eighteen year olds to vote. Separate organizations for young people allow them to function as organizations under the aegis of the parent organization. While junior members enjoy full membership rights as members of the junior organization, their organization is limited in its authority by the bylaws of both the parent organization and those of the junior organization.

Other classifications of members include associate members, active members, communicant members and the like. The scope of associate membership must be spelled out in the bylaws of the organization. Here it seems pertinent to point out that the bylaws authorize only what is included in them, there being no implied powers.

One church council in California, annoyed with its pastor, told him that ex officio membership did not permit his participation in council deliberations. Obviously there was an *ad hominem* interpretation directed against a pastor unsatisfactory in the eyes of the council; but personal antagonism may not displace bylaws authority, however strongly held by those who would substitute feelings for authority.

A president of a national veterans organization decided that she would replace area representation with nationwide at-large representation on the basis that the bylaws did not forbid her doing so; therefore, she could reorganize on her initiative as president. Of course, she was wrong, and her plan was disallowed.

Common sense dictates that every action of the officers of an organization cannot be spelled out. The officers are expected to be honorable people moved by the welfare of the organization they serve. Bylaws both specify what is valid, and by their silence, what is invalid; but no bylaws can require a president to be "hardworking, intelligent, sensitive to others feelings, available, and pleasant." These desirable characteristics must be discerned by the members before they vote in their officers. Obvious absence of these qualities will cause them to deny the officership to those lacking them.

Procedures for revocation of membership must be spelled out in the bylaws for they are indispensable to a healthy organization. Hopefully, they will not be used; but not having them can literally destroy an organization when fractious members refuse to carry out their responsibilities as members.

Standards of the organization impose on each member conduct that fosters the continuation of the organization. Habitual arguing with the chair or other members must be counterbalanced by bylaws that protect the organization from those who would destroy it by their insistence on having their own way. Ordinarily, bylaws provisions that spell out rights and duties of membership provide for removal of members unwilling to accept the responsibilities of membership.

An organization must lodge in its presiding officer the authority necessary to carry on proper meetings. Authority provided is not necessarily authority applied, but such authority must be available to the presiding officer and to the assembly.

There is the old story of the pioneer who had a hole in the roof of his cabin: When the sun was shining the hole made no difference; when it was raining, he couldn't repair it. So authority is provided not for the reasonable people, but for the unreasonable people; but it must be provided lest the unreasonable people destroy the organization whose leaders were too timid to act, or too blind to see what was happening.

Questions and Answers

Q: **Why should there be different kinds of membership? Isn't every member just as good as every other member?**
A: The organization may require different levels of membership because of age alone. Every organization has the authority to develop its own membership qualifications. Giving full membership to fifteen year olds is generally not wise.

Q: The pastor of a small midwestern church was angered by the council's developing a budget for the church during the pastor's absence. One council member said privately later, "Why's he mad? He ain't got nothing to do with the budget?" Was the member wrong?

A: Totally. As the leader of the church the pastor must participate in the development of the budget which is a blueprint for many of the church's activities for the upcoming fiscal year. As ex officio member of the council the pastor has a right to participate in the most important function of a church council except the calling of a pastor.

Underlying the ignorance of the member was a desire to concentrate power in the council by eliminating the pastor's input and influence. The pastoral leader of a church must participate in determining church policies or become a puppet who only preaches on Sunday and visits the sick.

Q: Why do organizations need bylaws? Can't people just cooperate without having a lot of bylaws they have to obey?

A: In the best of all worlds, perhaps bylaws would not be necessary. You seem to assume that there is only one way to do something, and that reasonable people can and will agree on that one way, but honest and dedicated people can disagree. There are many roads to Rome. Therefore, the underlying principle of organizations remains: Majority rules, with adequate protection of the rights of the minority.

CHAPTER XIV - Voting
On Votes and Voting

A member of a garden club said to me: "Counting votes always bothers me. Is there a quick way to count votes?"

There are four ways to count votes. The voice vote is determined by the volume of sound people make. Be careful that a loudmouthed minority doesn't prevail over a quieter majority. If you think the vote is not correctly understood by the chair, shout, "Division," and get a standing vote.

There are two kinds of standing vote: one that is counted, one that is not. It is better to count, but sometimes the vote is so lop-sided that counting is not necessary. Be sure, however, to have the "ayes" and the "nays" stand separately so that a fair judgment can be made. If the number of "ayes" and "nays" seems close, then count both the "ayes" and the "nays" and give that number to the assembly.

Sometimes, in a small group, it is practical to count raised hands. Require people to *stretch* their hands so that they won't be missed. One time at a garden club elections a hand-raised vote came out evenly, fifty to fifty. Doubting that vote, people were asked to stand and be counted. The second result was fifty-three to fifty.

If you are the chair, get two other people to count. If the two do not agree, have them recount. Then you, as the chair, announce the vote.

Any member can demand a standing vote, but the assembly must authorize a standing counted vote. Again, whenever in doubt, have a standing counted vote, and have two other people do the counting.

The most democratic way of voting is by ballot. The chair always votes - if a member - because the chair's ballot cannot be differentiated from any other ballot. The ballot is secret; no one knows how anyone else voted. Tellers must do the tabulating and then report to the chair.

Once a vote is taken it may not be retaken unless there was general confusion about the issue being voted on, or if fraud is discovered. If you are the chair be sure to explain what is being voted on before the vote. If you are a member and voting and do not understand the issue, ask. If you understand the issue, and know how you want to vote, be sure that you understand what "yes" and "no" mean in terms of the issue.

If you oppose a motion, vote against it even if you are the only one. Later, if you are proved to be right, you will receive credit from people who did not vote against the motion out of misinformation or fear of angering someone else.

Remember, you never have to justify your vote. If you are challenged, refer the person to the parliamentary authority that says your vote is private, and is your own business. If you are not sure of how you feel about the motion being voted on, abstain. Abstaining is a non-vote, not a "no" vote. If you abstain, your vote is added to the vote of the winning side.

So is there a quick way to count a vote? Yes, but only when appropriate. Voting is too important for quick counts.

Kinds of Votes

"But what kind of vote do I use?" wailed Samantha Sommerfeld, newly elected president of the Horse Owners Club. "I know about horses, how to buy them, but that gavel scares me."

What Samantha needs first is to prepare for the meeting, to write out the entire script for the meeting - as best she can. She needs to set up a written agenda, and to study the kinds of voting that may come up in a meeting.

Kinds of voting

1. **Voice** or *viva voce*: "All in favor say aye, opposed no . . . ."
2. **Show of hands:** "All in favor raise your hand high, opposed."
3. **Standing vote:** "All in favor please rise . . . ."
4. **Standing, counted votes:** "All in favor rise. Will the tellers please count the vote."
5. **Ballots:** "The tellers will circulate the ballots. Please write "yes" or "no" on your ballot."
6. **Unanimous or general consent:** Nobody objects.

The use of different kinds of voting

Voice or *viva voce* (veva voche) is used when the outcome of the vote is expected to be overwhelmingly positive. The first situation that comes to mind is the end of a long meeting. Adjournment can be achieved two ways:

A. A member may say, "I move adjournment," there is a second, and the chair says, "All in favor say 'aye.' Those opposed say 'no.' The 'ayes' have it, the meeting is adjourned."

OR

B. The chair may say, "There being no other business (pauses for three seconds), the meeting is adjourned."

The motion from the floor is the procedure with which most people are familiar. Generally, there is clear support for adjournment. However, the chair must ask for the negative vote; he may not skip it because the positive vote is overwhelming. When the chair asks for the negative vote perhaps no one votes against adjournment, but the chair must always preside conservatively. Later the Chair can expect people who were prevented from getting what they wanted to charge the chair with bias, with rushing to get the meeting over. Though the charge may not be true, it is best to avoid giving a disgruntled person the opportunity to charge the chair with improper presiding by presiding conservatively and firmly.

The second way to adjourn, announcement by the chair, is used when the chair feels all are in favor of a motion, in this case, adjournment. Silence means consent in this case. If no member objects, everyone agrees. If one person objects, a voice vote should be taken.

Raising of hands is sometimes effective in small meetings, rarely in large ones. If there are 15 people voting, raised hands permits an easy, accurate vote. (The chair should have at least one other person counting to ascertain that the count is accurate.)

If the meeting is large, over 50 people, counting raised hands frequently causes confusion. For example, I served as parliamentarian for the uniformed fire officers of New York City at a meeting where 200 members were present. A raised hands vote was taken. One hundred members voted for the motion, exactly 100 members voted against it. I was skeptical of the accuracy of the vote, not believing 200 people would vote precisely 50 percent for and 50 percent against.

Another vote was taken, this time with members standing. The vote was 103 to 97 in favor.

The trouble with the raised-hand vote is people raise their hands in different ways: some barely raise their hands over their heads, some put their hands down before they are counted, and other hands are overlooked because they are not stretched high enough to be counted. Not seeing some raised hands is certain when the members are moving around, chatting and twisting their bodies.

Any member may demand a standing vote simply by shouting out "Division" but he may not demand a standing, <u>counted</u> vote. He does not require the chair's recognition, and may interrupt a member who has the floor. The chair must stop all other action, and have the members who favor the motion stand, and then be seated. Next the members opposed stand, and then are seated.

The standing vote may easily be ascertained simply by looking at those voting aye, though the wise presider will also ask for the no vote. If the vote is indisputable, it is a waste of time to count individual members. However, the wise presider will have at least another person at the head table agree the positive vote is a clear majority.

Two possibilities arise from the reaction of the chair to the vote. The chair may be in doubt, or a member may be in doubt. Either way there is quick and easy remedy for resolution of the doubt.

The chair says, "The chair is in doubt. If there is no objection (pauses three seconds), there will be a standing, counted vote. Tellers, please count your assigned sections."

The member may say, "Mr. Chairman, I move for a standing counted vote." With a second and a majority support, a standing counted vote must be taken.

On Long Island at a meeting of Realtors, there was doubt about a vote. The house was physically divided into those favoring the motion and those opposed. As individual supporters of the motion left their group they were counted by the secretary and the parliamentarian. The standing counted vote sustained the earlier standing vote. Having done all that could be done to assure the correctness of the vote, no one who opposed the motion could charge the procedures were unfair or inaccurate.

Of all forms of voting, balloting has the advantage of being the most democratic and most private. The simplest form of balloting requires the writing the word "Yes" as the only word on the ballot, or the word "No" as the only word on the ballot.

Once, at a tennis umpires' meeting, a voice vote was held. Immediately one member challenged another member, saying, "Why did you vote for that motion?" The chair, being weak, said nothing; but the asking member should have been reprimanded. A basic parliamentary premise is no member may be required to justify his vote, nor can his vote be challenged. In a ballot vote, only the individual member knows how he or she voted.

Silly people sometimes confer with someone near them about how to vote. Such conferring vitiates the purpose of the ballot, secrecy and accuracy. If one member causes another to vote a particular way, the first member becomes more than one member (his vote plus influencing another vote), and the second person becomes less than a member (his vote becomes the other person's vote, not his.) *Discussing* with another person to *clarify* the question before voting is reasonable, but to ask another person how to vote aggrandizes one member and diminishes the other.

The presider, if a member, casts his ballot with the other members. Should there be a tie, the chair may not then vote again, for he would then have two votes. If a ballot is tied, then the motion is lost, a tie vote being a lost vote. The same motion may not be renewed in the same meeting unless it has been substantially changed.

What the proponents of the motion must do is to round up enough votes *before* the next meeting, renew the motion at the proper time during the meeting, and get the motion passed.

The same advice goes to the opponents of the motion, that is, to roundup votes in opposition, expecting the proponents to secure promises of support from members opposed or not present at the first meeting, and to renew the motion.

Parliamentary procedure provides the means for action, but not the will for action. The latter must come from persons knowledgeable of their rights, of parliamentary procedure, and a determination to see the assembly accept their points of view through actions of the assembly.

Of course, ballots are the only physical proof of the accuracy of a vote. How long should they be kept.? Sometimes bylaws require they be kept a specified period of time. For Florida condos, the time is one year. However, if there is no such provision, a good rule of thumb is to keep them under lock for 90 days. They can be reviewed by authority of the executive board, but no one person alone should ever review them. Any person handling ballots alone, however honorable that person may be, puts himself in the position of being suspected of, if not charged with, tampering.

A wise president thinks, "What could the most suspicious member who doesn't like me unreasonably say about my actions?" The wise president cannot stop criticism, but he or she can lessen that criticism by so acting that reasonable people will not believe unfair criticism leveled against the president, since proof cannot be provided to prove the criticism.

Unanimous or general consent simply means, "If you don't disagree, then you agree." Generally, the matter is so obviously preferred that time is saved by the chair's announcement. For example, "There being no objection, the assembly will recess for 20 minutes. We will restart at 2:20 P.M. (Pause for three seconds.) The chair, seeing no objection, declares a 20-minute recess."

The obvious vote is a voice vote. If a voice vote is unclear, then the chair had best consider not having a recess at that time. Taking a standing counted vote for a recess is overloading the situation. The chair could simply say, "There being doubt that the assembly wants to recess, we will continue."

If members have been inattentive when the chair proposed the doubtful recess, for example, then a member from the floor can move for a recess as a main motion, debatable, amendable, requiring a majority vote.

Frequently, a recess is proposed after protracted debate over a controversial or complex subject. Recess, being connected with a motion under debate, becomes a privileged motion, and is not debatable, but is amendable. For example, the time allotment may be considered too long or too short. The time allotment can be changed, and the amended motion then voted on. However, if recess is proposed when no other motion is under consideration, then recess is treated as any other main motion; that is, it is debatable and amendable and requires a majority vote for passage.

Informed voting is the heart of the parliamentary process. *Uninformed* voting weakens an organization. Abstention from voting can becomes the death knell of an organization.

Unanimous or General consent

What is known as "unanimous consent" carries with it certain anomalies that indicate the need for the more accurate term, "general consent."

The chair may ask, "If there is no objection to accepting the minutes as presented, (pause) the minutes are accepted." Lack of objection is not the same as support. If I do not respond to my son's request for a raise in his weekly allowance, it does not follow that I have agreed to give him a raise. However, if silence implies consent, then not objecting at the time the chair gives me opportunity to object means, functionally, I agree.

General consent attempts to eliminate that logical contradiction. However, the use of "general" can be interpreted as being majority, and thus can cause confusion where it seeks to spread light.

For the presider - and for the assembly - unanimous consent allows the assembly to get through routine business quickly and fairly. If there is erroneous material in the minutes, one person's objecting can usually get it corrected; then the chair can ask for unanimous consent for accepting the minutes "as corrected."

The rule of thumb is unanimous consent is used only when the question for which unanimous consent is asked provides no apparent controversy. However, if one member of the assembly objects, a majority vote taken by the chair is necessary for passage of the question before the assembly.

All four of the most prominent parliamentary authorities address unanimous consent, Demeter with many references in different places in his book; Robert with detailed explanations over many pages; Sturgis with a paragraph; and Keesey with an excellent explanation that merits quoting in full:

> Strictly speaking, a unanimous vote should mean that all members present and eligible to vote did so, and that all voted the same way. Some liberty is taken with the definition when a presiding officer announces a "unanimous decision" following a vote by general consent. To say that a member did not object is different than saying he voted. A more accurate announcement of the results of such a vote would be, 'The motion is carried without objection,' or 'The motion is carried without any dissenting votes.' When a member chooses not to vote and to abide by the decision formed by those who do vote, it is not accurate to announce a decision that suggests he did vote.
>
> It is recommended that the term 'by unanimous vote' not be used carelessly. Members may be offended, but not wish to protest its misuse openly. Organizations have been known to pass a motion by majority vote and then, under the impression it would look better on the record, agree to make the vote unanimous if no on objects. Very little sober reflection is needed to condemn this practice. It offends the basic principle of equality of membership, which guarantees each member the right to vote or abstain from voting without having to reveal which he did. The practice of declaring a member who is elected to office by secret ballot as 'elected by unanimous vote' if no one objects, fools no one and should be condemned. For the secretary to 'cast a unanimous ballot' for a candidate, even if he is unopposed, should never be condoned. A unanimous vote should mean just what it says (Keesey, p. 130).

Not only must unanimous consent be used carefully, it should never be used in controversial matters. There is a report of a church assembly that, having elected a new assistant pastor by majority vote, was asked to make the vote unanimous in order to show strong support for the new assistant pastor. Such a motion would obviously be made by a member of the prevailing side, the side that voted for the assistant pastor. However, there are two unfortunate ramifications from this well-intentioned motion. First, there is an appearance of unanimity where unanimity does not exist. Because those opposed to the new assistant have lost, it does not follow that defeat will immediately cause them to change their minds, and favor the new assistant pastor.

Second, there is an underlying power play that has the majority say, in effect, to the minority, "You lost the election, now change your mind and join us. Be good sports, and admit you lost." But the minority may prove to be right. Suppose the assistant pastor stays only a short time and leaves for any number of negative reasons, then the position taken by the minority is vindicated, and the judgment of the majority is proved wrong. "Being good sports?" An election of an assistant pastor is not a sporting event, and should not be treated as such.

There is an axiom in parliamentary procedure that a person may not be required to defend his vote. The motion for a unanimous vote asks a minority member to: 1) admit he was wrong in voting against the assistant pastor; 2) to bow down to the majority by changing his vote; and 3) to defend his vote.

It is not implied that a conspiracy - a popular American explanation for things that go against one's wishes - exists among the majority, that they proceeded with evil design. Probably the majority members just thought it "would be nice if we have a unanimous vote." And watching a child wave fireman matches around as if they were batons may be cute, but the inherent danger in the matches is the fire the matches can generate and the child's immaturity in realizing the danger of a struck match.

There are overtones to the forced unanimous vote that majority members can hardly perceive. After all, the majority members got their way; so what's all the fuss about? For the minority members, they have not only lost a vote and they feel as strongly in opposition to the new pastor as the majority feels support for him - they have been shown by actions of the majority that they were wrong and "poor sports" if they continued to hold their strongly held views. The greater problem is the discontent in the breasts of the minority members, a discontent that will ramify through their participation as members of the church. The insensitivity of the majority can cause the minority to feel affronted and misused, and in so feeling, the minority members can lessen their support for church programs and activities, and even cause them to leave the church.

The pitfalls above can be avoided by knowledge of parliamentary procedure firmly set on a foundation of empathy and concern for others. The golden rule is neither hackneyed nor cliche, but a reasonable means for living with others in social situations requiring individual discipline. Unfairness based on ignorance is nonetheless hurtful, and saying a vote is unanimous when it isn't - for whatever cosmetic reasons - carries the seeds of discord far greater than the unthinking presider imagines.

Questions and Answers

1. The president of our sailing club takes the positive vote on motions, but not the negative vote. Is that a type of unanimous consent?
Emphatically, no. The chair must always take both the negative and the positive vote, except in the commendation of the work of an outstanding person, for example, when the negative is not taken.

2. The president of our condo ends our meeting by saying, "If there is no more new business, the meeting is adjourned." He then raps the gavel and says, "The meeting is adjourned." Doesn't adjournment require a motion from the floor?

The president is right. If there is no more business and the meeting cannot continue without business - then the chair's closing the meeting is fair and time-saving. Adjournment does not require a motion from the floor, though most meetings are adjourned that way.

3. Why is unanimous consent so rarely used in meetings I attend?

Probably because it is not understood. It is a handy procedure used to reduce talk and time in meetings.

The Flawed Election of Manager Mutz - Almost

After weeks of indecision following the retirement of Manager Paul Kraus, the board of directors by a vote of 8 to 4 installed Paul Mutz, Kraus's assistant, as manager of Waving Palms, a 600-unit condo. There were those on the board who supported Mutz, those who opposed him, and those who liked him well enough, but thought that placing the current assistant in the role of manager was a mistake. After Mutz was elected manager, Mike Maxwell, a particularly ardent supporter of Mutz, addressed the chair.

Member Maxwell: I move the vote for Mutz be made unanimous.

Member Brown: Second.

Chair: The chair rules the motion out of order. It is out of order to ask for the record to show unanimous support for Mutz when a third of the board voted against him.

While the enthusiasm for unanimous support for Mutz is understandable, and shows great confidence in him, Mutz did not receive unanimous support. Thus an attempt to show a unanimous vote for him is inaccurate, and probably, illegal. The motivation for the request for a unanimous vote seems to be to show the world that now that Mutz had been elected, everyone supports him. Even if a member who voted against Mutz magnanimously moves to make the vote unanimous, he is being magnanimous with other people's votes. Magnanimity is one thing, grandstanding is another especially with other people's votes.

There are additional serious objections to asking for a unanimous vote. The fact that Mutz has been elected does not gainsay the fact that a third of the board voted against him. Because Mutz won does not mean that opposition to him should be papered over by a doubtful parliamentary procedure. On the contrary, the large opposition to him should inspire Mutz to win over the members opposed to him by excellent service to all members of the board. Certainly, to pretend that differences do not exist, or that the board now supports him unanimously, is illusory. For those who opposed Mutz's election, the motion for unanimous support is insulting. In effect, the motion says that those opposed are not worthy of consideration, now that Mutz has been elected by a majority.

But always implicit in the rule of the majority is the protection of the minority for the very good reason that those in the majority today may be in the minority tomorrow, and all should have their votes properly respected, whatever side of a question they take. New manager Mutz may be uncomfortable for he is being asked to accept a popular support that does not exist. Suppose that Member Maxwell's motion is carried by majority vote, then a majority of the board members forces the minority to deny their opposition, and to accept the will of the majority as their own with only a majority vote! The majority not only wins what it wants, but insists the losing minority agree with it! That is hardly democracy in action.

There is an echo here of the acclamation procedure, or the secretary's casting a unanimous vote. Both stifle free and open discussion of candidates' qualifications for office, adumbrating the victory of the successful candidate by pretending board unanimity.

New manager Mutz must concentrate on his election, not on the votes against him. In time he may learn who opposed him, but if he seeks too energetically to find out, he may alienate some of those who voted for him and will further justify the opposition of those who voted against him. He must, in short, accentuate the positive, go ahead confidently because he has board approval, and perform competently in his new role.

Voting for Church Council Membership

There are two obvious methods for electing church council members: Have the nominating committee present a slate of qualified people, one person for each opening; or, have the nominating committee present at least two or more persons for each opening.

Some church organizations find the first method - one person for each opening - a good one. The nominating committee has done a winnowing process whereby the best qualified people are asked to run, and are assured election. Of course, the members of the nominating committee must be carefully selected, representing the different constituencies that make up the church's membership, and exemplifying intelligence, maturity, balance, and devotion to the welfare of the congregation. When, therefore, a person is asked to fill an opening by standing for election, that person has survived one winnowing process directly by the nominating committee and indirectly through council choice of nominating committee members.

There is a down side to this process. Some voting members feel that the process is basically undemocratic, that their vote will not affect the outcome of the election. They consider themselves rubber stamps for the nominating committee - and no one likes to be a rubber stamp.

Robert counsels against having the report of the nominating committee be the election slate for reasons outlined above. In addition, there must always be opportunity for nominations from the floor; but the chances of a nomination from the floor defeating a person selected by the nominating committee are slim to none - unless the nominating committee has been obviously biased in its selection of nominees.

The other method is to require at least two names for each opening on the council. For the moment, let us consider requiring three or more names for each opening. Requiring three or more names for each opening can easily generate confusion among the voting members. The prospect of an election ballot of nine members' names for three openings can be confusing. The perusal of such a ballot confirms the possible confusion.

As always, the will of the group being served must determine the method of nominations/election. However, the group must know that a very capable person, asked to sacrifice to serve on a council, may not be voted down casually. That capable person may never thereafter be available to the work of the organization, not because of the sting of defeat, but because of the realization that his fellow members feel he has insufficient capacity to be a council member. It is then the organization will suffer the loss of a capable person for reasons as absurd as a slavish devotion to democratic processes taken to the extreme that makes them unfair, a greater devotion to process than to the persons chosen, and a lack of recognition of past and present services rendered to the organization in deference to providing a number of candidates for whom members can vote.

Church council membership is particularly sensitive. People are asked to serve in demanding positions of trust, without compensation, and without adequate recognition of the demands of the positions, with real possibilities of personal attacks because of actions taken by the church council. When defeat which must happen to three of the six candidates nominated for three open positions is added to the reluctance of busy, capable people to serve, the result can be devastating to the individuals who lose, and to the council upon which they would have served had they been elected.

Both methods of election are used. If either is used consistently, it is better than using one method one year, and the other method the following year. There is then a mixture of the board of members who could not be defeated, and people who survived the multiple-choice election process.

This writer's opinion is that selection of the nominees by the nominating committee - with opportunity to nominate from the floor - is the better process for church councils.

Tellers Tabulating Tallies -- Another Method

The annual meeting of the Church of the Cross went smoothly - as usual. There were the reports of the various chairmen, and the annual budget was presented - as usual. The budget showed modest increases - as expected. But what was additional for this annual meeting was the report of the Building Committee, recommending the construction of the new sanctuary, at a cost of over a million dollars. With the aid of an overhead projector, the Building Committee members presented the drawings, and explanations of the proposed new sanctuary - with anticipated costs. Nothing unusual here, except for the tabulating of the ballots that would determine the construction of the new sanctuary.

At first, that tabulating appeared usual. Three women took the stack of ballots into the kitchen, and separated them into piles of yesses and noes - but then the innovation!

Cindy Hamilton, the head teller, had been told the best method of counting ballots - as all parliamentarians know. And that method is to tabulate the vote in bunches of five's - IIII - then count the bunches of fives. But Cindy had a better idea.

On each yes ballot she wrote a number in the lower right hand corner, thusly: "One," she said aloud, writing "I" in the lower right hand corner. "Two," writing "2" in the lower right hand corner. "Three," she said, writing "3" in the lower right hand corner.

So she proceeded, calling each progressively higher number aloud as she wrote that number in the lower right hand corner of each ballot as she counted it.

What she was doing was tabulating as she counted. By counting aloud, writing that same number on the ballot, she was carrying on a simultaneous check of the accuracy of her count, and getting immediate verification from the other tellers who were watching and listening to her.

She placed the counted 107 yes ballots in three piles for convenience. On each ballot was the number she had assigned to it. And the small piles allowed her and the other tellers easy handling of the 3"x3" ballots.

The no votes - having previously been segregated - were easy to count, there being only six of them. Because there were only six no votes, they were not tabulated, only counted.

Advantages of Counting and Tabulating at the Same Time

1. One step - the writing down of the groups of fives - was eliminated, thus speeding up the count.
2. Possible errors in transferring the audible count to paper count were precluded by writing down the counted number as the tabulating number.
3. Any slip in the audible count would have been noticed immediately by the other tellers.
4. The sequence of audible/written numbers served as a check on possible mistakes by the head teller. For instance, the head teller would hardly jump from, say, 15 to 17 aloud, and then write down 16 on the ballot. Were she to do so, her error would have been noticed immediately.
5. The computation was swift, the total tabulating taking less than ten minutes.
6. The parishioners waited only ten minutes for the count of the ballots.

7. The tellers were perfectly sure the count was right. There was no point to a re-count.
8. Every ballot had a written number in the lower right hand corner, allowing easy checking as to proper sequence of the numbers used.

Disadvantages to the Tabulation Process

1. Practically, only one person can count aloud and tabulate at the same time. Thus, the process may not be practical with a large number of ballots. It may be possible for two head tellers to count aloud and tabulate, aided by two sets of tellers, but there would be a need for different rooms to avoid possible confusion about the numbers being said aloud, and the two sets of numbers would have to be put together.
2. No re-checking the tabulation may raise some doubts, especially among those who voted no.

This innovative tabulating process was accepted easily by the other tellers, and by the parishioners. Such acceptance is easily understood when one considers how common-sensical the procedure is.

Cindy Hamilton was surprised that anyone should be impressed by her simple tabulating process, which exemplified honest and verifiable count, with minimum time in processing the one hundred thirteen ballots.

The vote was 94.6% in favor of building the new sanctuary.

Preferential Balloting - An Election

Last year the election for the Garden Club presidency was so acrimonious that the Garden Club almost disbanded. This year one soon explained the advantages of preferential voting to the other members so persuasively that preferential voting was made a part of the bylaws, with the consequence that this year voting for the presidency became an orderly procedure for the Garden Club members.

One hundred ballots were distributed to elect a president. The names of five candidates appeared on each ballot. Each member was instructed to vote for no more than five names -IN ORDER OF PREFERENCE - to place 1 before his first choice, 2 before his second choice, 3 before his third choice, 4 before his fourth choice, and 5 before his fifth choice. The first candidate to receive 51 votes, composed of 51 first preferences, OR a combination of first preferences and enough second, third, fourth, and fifth choices to make 51, would be elected president.

The First Counting

Member Able	40
Member Baker	25
Member Carley	15
Member Dodd	12
Member Early	8

The 40 ballots for Member Able as first choice were put in one pile; the 25 votes for Member Baker were placed in a second pile; the 15 votes for Member Carley were placed in a third pile; the 12 votes for Member Dodd were placed in a fourth pile; the 8 votes for Member Early were placed in a fifth pile.

The 8 votes for Member Early were distributed among the piles of the four remaining candidates, according to <u>second</u> choices on the Early ballots.

The Second Counting

Member Able	40 + 4 = 44
Member Baker	25 + 2 = 27
Member Carley	15 + 1 = 16
Member Dodd	12 + 1 = 13

The 13 votes for Member Dodd were distributed among the piles of the three remaining candidates.

The Third Counting

Member Able	40 + 4 + 4 = 48
Member Baker	25 + 2 + 7 = 34
Member Carley	15 + 1 + 2 = 18

The 18 votes for Member Carley were distributed between the piles of Member Able and Member Baker.

The Fourth Counting

Member Able   40 + 4 + 4 + 10 = 58
Member Baker   25 + 2 + 7 + 8 = 42

MEMBER ABLE WINS WITH A MAJORITY OF THE 100 BALLOTS CAST

Care must be taken by the tellers to place the second, third, and fourth choices on top of the first choices for the remaining candidates. The total piles are then counted, including all votes, first, second, third, and fourth choices for the remaining candidates.

An analysis of the balloting for Member Able shows that 40 people got their first preference; four people got their second preference; four people got their third preference; and 10 people got their fourth preference.

If there is a tie between the remaining two candidates, the candidate with the greater number of first preferences wins.

Preferential voting is permitted only as it is set up in the bylaws.

Advantages to preferential balloting are it:
1. Requires only one balloting;
2. Is particularly good when voting by mail is involved.

Disadvantages to preferential balloting are:
1. Voting members cannot change their minds;
2. Democratically, it is less preferable than repeated balloting. In a third or fourth balloting, Member Carley might win as compromise candidate.

The greatest advantage to preferential balloting is that it permits members to cast one vote, rather than the repeated votes that would be required if all candidates stayed on the ballot until one achieved a majority.

It is self-evident that repeated balloting would be:
1. expensive;
2. time-consuming;
3. likely to lessen the number of returned ballots as members became weary of repeated balloting;
4. likely to result in less than the necessary majority vote.

The winner of the repeated balloting may have less than a majority vote of the total membership, thereby causing conflict with bylaws provisions, minority officership, and the mathematical possibility that more members voted against the winner than voted for him. Still, preferential balloting plays a pivotal role in voting in the situation described above.

Preferential Balloting - An Issue

Florida condo law requires that financial reserves be considered before the adoption of each condo's annual budget. The condo unit owners may opt to set up:

1. 100% of reserves,
2. 50% of reserves, or
3. 0% of reserves

Condos in Florida can use all three options; but whatever the option used by an individual condo, that option must have been authorized by a majority of the condo unit owners. A complication to securing the support of the majority of condo unit owners is the absentee ownership of many Florida condo units. How best then to secure the support of absentee owners? The preferential ballot may be the answer.

All 100 unit owners, present and away, receive ballots with the following instructions:

Prioritize the three choices below, putting 1 before your first choice, 2 before your second choice, and 3 before your third choice.

When the ballots have been received, the first choices are put in three piles:

First Tally
100% of reserves	20
50% of reserves	48
0% of reserves	32

Since the fewest number opted for 100% reserve, those twenty ballots are distributed to the remaining piles, according to the **second** choices on the 100% reserves ballots.

Second Tally
50% of reserves	48 + 12 = 60
0% of reserves	32 + 8 = 40

Three-fifths of the owners voted for 50% of reserves. Of the hundred owners who voted, 48 got their first choice, and 12 got their second choice.

There are advantages to preferential balloting:
1. It requires only one balloting;
2. It is particularly good when a mail ballot is involved.

There are also disadvantages to preferential balloting:
1. Voting members cannot change their votes;
2. It is less democratic than repeated ballots, using all three options. It precludes the possibility that owners voting for 100% reserves might win on repeated ballots, for their first choice was wiped out.

The greatest advantage to preferential balloting is that it permits members to cast one vote, rather than the repeated votes that would be required if the three options stayed on the ballot.

It is self-evident that repeated balloting would be:
1. expensive;
2. time consuming;
3. likely to lessen the number of returned ballots as members became weary of repeated balloting;
4. likely to result in less than the necessary majority vote.

The option finally chosen may enjoy less than a majority vote of the owners, thereby causing conflict with bylaws provisions, minority officership, and the mathematical possibility that more owners voted against 50% than voted for them. Still, preferential balloting can play a pivotal role in specific situations; if the bylaws authorize preferential balloting.

Plurality Voting

"A plurality vote is the largest number of votes to be given any candidate or proposition when three or more - choices are possible" (Robert, p. 399).

In the political field, one example of large scale plurality voting is the election of the mayor of the City of New York. After his second campaign, John Lindsay received 37% of the votes cast - meaning that almost 2 out of 3 persons in the election voted **against** Lindsay - still he was elected mayor. New York City had previously opted to use plurality voting because more than two candidates usually ran for mayor.

While it is axiomatic in parliamentary procedure that a majority elects a person, or adopts a motion, a plurality is perceived as needed in certain circumstances, authorization for preferential voting being spelled out in the bylaws. In non-legislative organizational arenas, plurality voting is seldom used, except perhaps in the case of national organizations. The incontrovertible fact is a person elected by a majority has had more persons vote **for** him than **against** him. A person elected by a plurality has had more persons vote **against** him than **for** him.

The difference between a majority vote for candidate and a plurality vote for a candidate is subtle, for the plurality winner is just as much elected as the majority winner. As George Will wrote, "He (Clinton) won 100 percent of the White House."

An example of majority and plurality votes shows up clearly in the elected bodies of the United Kingdom and Israel: the majority party in the United Kingdom selects its leader who becomes Prime Minister. Since there is no majority party in Israel, there must be a coalition of the largest party with members of at least one other party in order to have a majority in the Knesset. If the Prime Minister in the UK is dismissed by his majority party, his party simply elects another Prime Minister. If the head of the government in Israel loses the support of the other party that gives it a majority in the Knesset, new elections must be held - unless another coalition can be put together.

It is charged that President Clinton does not have a clear mandate because he did not win a majority of the popular vote cast. On the other hand, he won a dear majority in the Electoral College. President Clinton points out that Abraham Lincoln won the presidency with only 39% of the vote, and no one doubts the legitimacy of Lincoln's election.

Plurality voting is not as clear cut as majority voting, but it is just as binding, and can be the only means for determining the winner of an election in some situations.

Mail Balloting

As Chairman of the Nominations Committee, you are charged with getting as many owners as you can to vote in upcoming election for the new board for your condo. The election promises to be a lively one, there being candidates on both sides of the issue of expanding condo property, some wanting to buy an adjoining parcel, others adamantly opposed to buying it. To insure the most reactions to the issues, you are determined to get as many owners to vote as you can get. What do you do?

First, you know that half the owners will be prevented from voting in person the night of the elections because they will be living elsewhere, and some may be ill. But they will be well enough to receive and answer mail - so you and your committee decide on a mail ballot.

You have the list of names of the candidates and the positions for which they are running distributed to the owners. You leave enough space at the bottom of the printed ballot so that qualified members' names can be written in, because you know that any member's name may be written in, even though not nominated.

With the ballot, you enclose a small envelope - 6-1/2" x 3-5/8." On that envelope you write instructions in capital letters, "MARK YOUR BALLOT. VOTE FOR NO MORE THAN FIVE PEOPLE OR YOUR BALLOT WILL BE DISCARDED. YOU MAY WRITE IN THE NAMES OF QUALIFIED PEOPLE BUT YOU MAY VOTE FOR NO MORE THAN FIVE PEOPLE. PLACE YOUR MARKED BALLOT INTO THIS ENVELOPE AND SEAL IT."

Separate the following instructions from the above by at least an inch on the front of the envelope. Then write: "PLACE THIS SEALED ENVELOPE - *WITHOUT A STAMP* - INTO THE ENCLOSED, LARGE, *STAMPED*, ADDRESSED ENVELOPE AND MAIL IT."

The directions may appear curt, but they are clear, and clarity is vital if this mail ballot is going to be successful.

Insure that the names on the outside of the stamped envelopes are checked against the list of owners qualified to vote, thus assuring that no owner votes twice, by mail and in person.

Have committee members slit the envelopes, putting the outside envelopes in one pile, and the envelopes holding the ballots in another pile, unopened.

Next, slit the envelopes holding the ballots, remove the ballots, and place them in a pile.

Have two people tabulate: the person on the left picks up a ballot, reads the member's choices aloud, then tabulates the votes on his blank master ballot, adding the write-in votes at the bottom of the master ballot. The second person, on the right, tabulates exactly the same as the other person. A third person, a teller, standing behind the two, observes the tabulating to insure accuracy.

After the tabulating is completed, the two tabulators, and the teller, compare the two master sheets, and ascertain the totals agree. The master sheets are then given to the parliamentarian/secretary team.

The nominating committee chairman reads the report, one office at a time. At the conclusion of the report for each office, the chair declares the winner, by saying, for example, "I declare Betty Ann Seger president."

The same pattern is followed for each office individually, the nominations chairman reading out the totals, the chair declaring the winners.

The chair then thanks the nominating committee and all others who helped in the nominations/elections process.

It is recommended that the counting of the ballots take place while the current president is carrying out the meeting agenda so that a recess for the counting does not extend the meeting too long. Further, by announcing the new officers at the end of the meeting, the new officers can take over immediately. There is value in having the outgoing president present the gavel to the incoming president, giving time for congratulations and the pleasantries that usually accompany a change in the board of directors.

Of course the new officers could take office after the adjournment of the meeting, but an opportunity to provide continuity of leadership would thereby be missed. By waiting, confusion can arise among the owners as to the precise time at which the new board takes office.

The purpose of elections is to insure that the majority of the owners decide who the new officers will be.

There is an axiom in parliamentary procedure that one takes the time and the effort to insure against possible upset through oversight of a procedural necessity. Sometimes owners in small condos reject the necessity of following strict rules in nominations and elections, thinking them needlessly burdensome; but later revealed irregularities may prove upsetting, and cause discord that could have been avoided by strict application of proper procedures. Smallness does not justify informality and lack of structure.

As nominations chairman, you must carry out the best plan you can secure. Your plan must answer two questions: Is it fair? Is it democratic? If the answer to both questions is yes, be easy in your mind, for the fair results of the election will remain after the carping criticism of the malcontents is forgotten. It is far better to look for and avoid irregularities that may cast an election in doubt than to speed up the election process to save time.

Questions and Answers

1. **I think your plan's too complicated. Why can't you just take the ballots and tabulate them without all the checking. Don't you trust the nominating committee?**
People make mistakes. The plan above cuts down on mistakes by having safeguards and more people involved. The honest person welcomes close scrutiny of what he does.

2. **Why must the chair announce the winners? Why not have the chairman of the nominating committee announce them?**
The status of the chair must be preserved. It is the chair's responsibility to announce the winners, and the chair must fulfill the responsibilities of the chair.

3. **Is every vote so important?**
Yes. I know a woman who was elected to a national position by a vote of 390 to 389. There was so much confidence in the election committee that the vote was not challenged. Can you imagine how the second woman felt, especially when she knew that of the two hundred delegates who had gone home early, some would have voted for her?

4. Are you saying that the nominating committee must do extra work to insure that no one challenges the results of an election?
Absolutely - whatever time and effort a fair election takes.

5. Are elections in a small organization so important?
Answer: Maybe even more so than in a large organization. The smaller the organization, the greater the concentration of power in the officers. Also, the election process must be so good that no one challenges the right of each officer to serve as an officer.

CHAPTER XV - Unusual Procedures
Rescind

There is an interesting parallel between Rescind and Amend Something Previously Adopted; both have an identical series of letter and numbers connected with their identification: M/BSDA2/3R/N. Interpreted, M/B means the motion is a main motion that brings a question again before the assembly; S means second; D means debate; A means amend; 2/3 means a two-thirds vote is required for passage; and R/N means only the negative can be reconsidered (Robert, p. 78).

Alice Sturgis takes a more liberal stance in the vote to adopt the motion to rescind. She requires only a majority vote, though she stipulates ". . . a motion that required more than a majority vote to pass can be rescinded only by the same vote that was required to approve it" (Sturgis, p. 44).

Interestingly, three prominent parliamentary authorities take three different positions concerning amending the motion to rescind: Robert (p. 300) says rescind may be amended by lessening the part to be rescinded, but cannot exceed that part; Sturgis (p. 44) says flatly the motion may not be amended; Keesey (p. 7) concurs with Robert in restricting amending to the part of the motion to be rescinded.

Clearly, rescind is a motion whose nature creates problems, starting with its unique and troubled classification, and continuing with its implementation, both in the vote required for its passage and the degree to which it can be amended.

The authorities agree that an adopted motion under which action has been taken may not be rescinded. Keesey (p. 78) gives the example of the attempt to rescind a decision made the previous fall to award an honorary degree to a person at the June graduation. One member objected, saying that considerable publicity had been given to the proposed award, and the recipient had agreed to accept the degree. Therefore, rescind was not in order.

Simplified, Rescind goes back into the minutes of previous meetings and expunges some portion of those minutes. The expunged portion is not literally erased, but has a line neatly drawn through it so that both the portion expunged, and the corrected entry can be read. Expunging and erasing are not synonymous.

Rescind goes back in the minutes and **expunges** a portion of the minutes.

Amend Something Previously Adopted goes back in the minutes and **corrects** a portion of the minutes.

Hillsdale Garden Club, June 15, 1991

Chairman: The chair recognizes Mr. Benedict Keen.

Mr. Keen: Mr. Chairman, the minutes of the January meeting show that I support the use of commercial fertilizers for the flowers. Mr. Chairman, I oppose the use of commercial fertilizers, and I ask that parts of the minutes of the January meeting that says I support commercial fertilizers for growing flowers be rescinded.

Secretary: I checked the minutes, Mr. Chairman. They show clearly Mt. Keen favored commercial fertilizers.

Mr. Keen: I didn't say that.

Secretary: Well, somebody said it.

Mr. Keen: Well, it wasn't me, and I want the record corrected.

Chairman: Please, ladies and gentlemen, there is an easy solution for this minor problem. Is there objection to having the secretary strike through that portion that states Mr. Keen favors commercial fertilizers? The chair, seeing no objection, rules . . . .

Mr. Dull: I object.

Chairman: Since objection has been raised, it will be necessary to have a vote. (Chair takes a rising counted vote.) A minimum 2/3 vote satisfies all the parliamentary authorities.

There is no statute of limitations on either Rescind or Amend Something Previously Adopted, and assemblies will ordinarily grant the request of the member allegedly misquoted. The situation becomes sticky if the member has changed his mind since the meeting, and wants the minutes changed to reflect his present conviction. While several members may be ready to insist that Mr. Keen did indeed favor the use of commercial fertilizer, what must be considered is the trauma for the organization that may ensue from refusing Mr. Keen's insistence that the minutes reflect what he said.

What difference does it make if Mr. Keen's request to rescind his statement is not accurately based? Mr. Keen thinks his statement is accurate. Is it not better to let Mr. Keen have his way since changing his vote does not change the stated position of the Garden Club?

Common sense and tolerance of human weakness both have a place. A strict, harsh insistence on total accuracy in a trivial matter may be too high a price to pay for tranquillity in the club. The larger picture of the general good must be measured against absolute accuracy by the chair.

Probably the knowledge that past error in minutes can be corrected is more important than correcting the error, for most errors are relatively trivial. However, if a person's integrity or reputation is involved, then the error in the minutes must be eliminated.

Questions and Answers

1. Why not go back in the minutes and white out the error and put the correction on top of the White-Out?
The original record should be kept, even though it has been judged to be inaccurate. The correction has been made and inserted in the minutes. Mr. Keen, in this case, will have to be satisfied with the corrected minutes.

2. Why use rescind only? Why not annul or repeal?
Rescind has been settled on as the word to use. However, apparently for clarity's sake, annul and repeal are recognized. Robert lists "Rescind. Repeal, or Annul" in his tinted pp: but the three terms appear only under Rescind.

3. Suppose someone wants to rescind something he said in the past that has now embarrassed him. Upon his request, should what he said be rescinded?
No, as tempting and innocuous as the request may be. Members must be responsible for what they say, and expect to be held accountable for it. One caution: the chair must be careful not to be

trapped into asking for unanimous consent for rescinding simply on a member's assertion of what he said. If not completely sure, the chair should temporize by saying, for example, "The chair and the secretary will investigate this matter and report to the club at the next regular meeting." When in doubt, the chair should not act.

4. Can the motion to rescind the abused?
Easily. A group can get into the bad habit of carefully perusing past minutes, looking for minute errors, and move that they be removed. Common sense must prevail. The chair must overrule abuse of the motion. The overrule of the chair can be appealed, but the overrule probably will be sustained by the assembly.

5. Who cares what year-old minutes say?
You care if you are misquoted and are embarrassed by what the minutes say.

Correcting Minutes

Linda: (to her friend Ellen) Do you know what that crazy secretary did? She recorded that in the November meeting I voted to *buy* a new computer for the club office when you know I voted **not** to buy one. What can I do?

Ellen: I don't think you can do anything. That meeting took place two months ago. The minutes of that meeting were approved in December, and this is January. But what do you care? The new computer wasn't approved anyway.

Linda: I'm glad we didn't buy the stupid thing, but I don't like being on record approving it.

Ellen: Well, there's nothing you can do now.

Was Ellen right? No, she was not. There is recourse open to Linda: **Amend Something Previously adopted.**

At the next regular meeting, Linda can move under *unfinished business* that the minutes be corrected. The procedure for that is **M/BSDA 2/3 R/N**. The formula, broken down, means: M/B is the category, meaning motions that bring a question again before the assembly; S means the motion must be seconded; A means the motion can be amended; 2/3 means at least two out of every three voters must approve; R/N means that only the negative can be reconsidered.

Linda: Mr. Chairman, I move to amend the November minutes to show that I voted *against* the motion to buy a new computer for the club office. The November minutes show that I voted *for* the new computer.

Chair: You've heard the motion. Is there a second?

Ellen: Second.

Chair: If there is no objection, the chair directs the secretary to change the November minutes as requested. (Pauses) The chair seeing no objection, directs the secretary to make the desired change.

Comments

The chair wisely used unanimous consent instead of calling for a standing vote by the assembly, if not a standing *counted* vote. It would be strange for the members not to be willing to correct the record. In this case, every member agreed. If one member had not agreed, the chair would probably take a standing, counted vote.

There is no need to assess blame for what is purportedly the secretary's error. There is the possibility that Linda did mistakenly vote for the motion, or that Linda changed her mind later. But, in order to promote harmony, there is sufficient reason to accept Linda's word, and simply change the minutes.

There is no time limit on amending something previously adopted. The record can be changed years after an erroneous entry, provided at least 2/3 of the assembly agrees to do so.

Physically, the secretary draws a neatly inked line through the original entry in the minutes so that it can still be read. Then the secretary writes the correction in brackets nearby.

There are two related motions, *Reconsider*, and *Rescind* (annul, repeal).

Questions and Answers

1. Why have I never heard of Amend Something Previously Adopted before?
It is obscure, and rarely used. However, it is a guarantee against the perpetuation of perceived error. Error that could prove damaging or embarrassing to the member wrongly quoted.

2. Why not just rescind the error in the minutes?
Rescind would wipe out the person's vote. It would eliminate the error, but would not state the member's correct vote.

3. What does R/N mean?
It means if the assembly votes no, the no vote can be reconsidered; but if the assembly votes yes, the vote may not be reconsidered.

4. Why is this so complicated? Why can't the assembly just go back and correct the error by a majority vote?
There's always the desire for simplicity; but simple solutions do not solve complex problems. If it were simple to change the minutes of the past, there could be the temptation to try to change minutes frequently, with a resulting frustrated feeling that nothing was ever final. The purpose of parliamentary procedure is to guarantee correctness and fairness. Oversimplifying and saving time have little importance compared with the necessary security members feel when business is considered predictably and according to parliamentary authority. The time required later in correcting error caused by too much haste is usually far greater than the time saved by moving too quickly originally.

5. If Amend Something Previously Adopted is so rarely used, why should it be considered at all?
By analogy, up to this point I have not needed life insurance; but I don't propose to give it up just because I have not needed it yet. So, a motion rarely used is not thereby useless. In my years as a parliamentarian I have never seen Amend Something Previously Adopted used; but like my life insurance - which is also necessary - it is a necessary motion.